DELIVERING
a course

The Complete Guide to Teaching a Course
Ian Forsyth, Alan Jolliffe and David Stevens

Planning a Course
Preparing a Course
Delivering a Course
Evaluating a Course

DELIVERING
a course

Practical
Strategies
for
Teachers,
Lecturers
and Trainers

**Ian Forsyth, Alan Jolliffe
and David Stevens**

Second Edition

**KOGAN
PAGE**

First published in 1995
Second edition 1999

Kogan Page Limited
120 Pentonville Road
London N1 9JN
UK

Stylus Publishing Inc.
22883 Quicksilver Drive
Sterling, VA 20166
USA

© Ian Forsyth, Alan Jolliffe and David Stevens, 1995, 1999

British Library Cataloguing in Publication Data

A CIP record for this book is available from the British Library.

ISBN 0 7494 2809 0

Typeset by Jean Cussons Typesetting, Diss, Norfolk
Printed and bound in Great Britain by Biddles Ltd, Guildford and King's Lynn

Contents

Introduction

The focus of this edition is the delivery of a course and course materials. This is the point where the planning and development reach the client, the learner, and are seen by the wider community.

In all of the four books in this series the possibility of overlap has to be recognized. After all 'planning' involves considerations of 'development' and 'delivery' and 'evaluation'. This book reflects on the planning and development stages but focuses on the reality of the delivery of the course and course materials.

Like the other books in this series this book recognises the existence of the World Wide Web and its increasing use in the delivery of learning materials. In this regard two new chapters have been added. Chapter 9 provides an in-depth review of computer managed learning and Chapter 10 looks at the use of the Web in the delivery of learning materials.

WHAT DOES EACH CHAPTER COVER?

Chapter 1 reviews the strategies needed at the delivery stage to open up a closed teaching setting. We recognize that teaching in a different manner may cause concerns for the students and the educational community. Chapter 2 discusses doing something different in teaching and learning, and addressing learners' concerns about their learning.

Chapter 3 addresses ways to promote acceptance of new teaching and learning strategies and materials. In this chapter the information in the planning and development stages outlined in the first two books in the series – *Planning a Course* and *Preparing a Course* – is reinforced.

Chapter 4 is about expecting the unexpected. It is based on 'Murphy's Law', in that if anything can go wrong it will.

Chapter 5 discusses what you will need to do prior to and during the delivery of teaching and learning materials so that the learner is able to accept new or different delivery techniques.

Chapter 6 describes the 'tell–show–do' aspects of the typical learning event and how each learning event can be structured to ensure learning takes place.

Chapter 7 looks at how the interaction between the learner and the teacher can be built into learning materials.

Chapter 8 discusses some of the issues raised by the growing expertise of the learner, prior experiences and the issues of electronic technology as an alternative source of information for learners.

Chapter 9 is an in-depth discussion of the use of computer managed learning (CML) in the tracking of the learner through a series of distance delivered or self study learning events. The chapter discusses learner interaction with CML, CML and open learning and provides you with a sample course map.

Chapter 10 introduces the idea of theWorld Wide Web as a library of learning resources as well a presenter and processor of learning materials. The chapter describes the advantages and disadvantages of the Web as a classroom tool for learning and reviews some of the design and development issues that will need consideration prior to the delivery of learning materials via the Web.

Overarching these chapters is the need for appropriate and accurate planning; also the need for various cost-effective delivery strategies, and analysis of these strategies by an assessment of the learning and thus the effectiveness of delivery.

Ian Forsyth
Alan Jolliffe
David Stevens

Chapter 1
Opening Up a Closed Setting

SUMMARY

This chapter describes both the open and closed classroom setting, the open learning continuum and the infrastructure you will need to support the open learning environment you create, along with some ways you can open up a closed setting.

INTRODUCTION

If you are teaching in a closed setting environment such as traditional mass instruction for example, you may think that there is no way you have either the time or the resources to develop a more open learning environment. However, there are a number of relatively simple ways you can open up a closed setting without major changes to the learning environment you are working in, without upsetting the institution's administration and, most importantly, without creating undue work for yourself.

A closed learning setting defined

The closed learning setting is probably the one with which you are most familiar; it's probable that you were educated in one. In a closed setting learners have little choice about what or how they learn as there is no flexibility in either the teaching or the learning environment. The learners progress in lockstep manner (fixed at a predetermined rate) and the teacher decides the rate of progress based on the

You were probably educated in a closed setting, so use that experience as a guide when you are developing your open learning materials.

length of the term or semester. Learners must pass examinations and wait a set period of time before they can progress to the next level.

In this type of setting those who learn more quickly are held back because they have to proceed at the same rate as the rest of the class, even if they have achieved all the required objectives. In some cases this may lead to boredom, possibly misbehaviour. In this setting the slower learners also have to proceed at the rate of the group even though they are not achieving all the required objectives. If the learning rate is too rapid the learners may fail their examinations and have to repeat the course. This often leads to learner disenchantment, or being labelled by others as 'remedial learners' leading to other adverse effects.

Traditional education is usually conducted in a closed setting. The teaching strategy used here is one of mass instruction using a lecture or tutorial delivery suited to large groups and a lockstep method of progress. Typically in a closed setting no recognition is given for prior learning by the learner, be it a formal qualification or some form of work experience. All learners are required to go through the same instruction in the same period of time.

An open learning setting defined

As you develop your open learning materials remember to take the characteristics of the learner into account.

In open learning settings the learners are able and encouraged to work at their own rate. They are given some choices in terms of their learning materials, learning styles, and the location of where some of their learning takes place. In many cases their prior learning is also recognized.

An open learning setting allows the learning environment to be freed of some of the more traditional constraints of education and makes learning more learner-centred. In other words, the characteristics of the learners become paramount rather than the concerns of the teachers, as is the case in a closed setting.

The open learning continuum

No education system can be said to be completely open or closed. The 'openness' of the system should be thought of as a continuum, as shown in Figure 1.1. Traditional education is shown at the closed end of the continuum and associated with delivery techniques such as mass instruction, while more open settings are associated with a more individualized instruction process.

Open learning infrastructure

One of the problems of implementing an open setting is developing a support infrastructure. In a closed setting less infrastructure is required because the teacher has greater control. When you have an open setting an effective management infrastructure has to be provided for the learner, that includes both resource management and learner support.

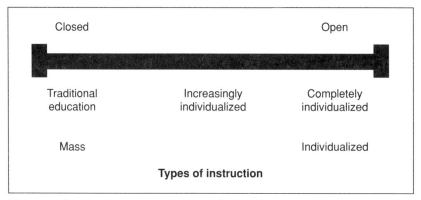

Figure 1.1   *The open learning continuum*

Greater support is required in an open learning setting because more is learned from the instructional materials than from the teacher. Learners may also need assistance to help them cope in the new learning environment.

RESOURCE MANAGEMENT

In an open learning setting instructional materials play a major role in helping learners to learn. These materials must be managed and maintained to ensure that they are appropriate and available to the learners when needed.

For the purposes of resource management, materials can be divided into four basic categories:

● print
● audio-visual
● computer
● real items.

Typical print materials are:

- chalkboards
- magnetic boards
- posters
- handouts

- self-instruction booklets
- assignments
- textbooks
- photos.

Audio-visual materials include:

- overhead transparencies
- radio and television broadcasts
- tape and text programmes
- filmstrips

- audio-tapes
- audio-discs
- slides
- videotapes.

Also included in this group is the equipment needed to 'play' these materials, and these must also be managed to ensure that they are operational and available to the learners when required.

Computer-based materials can include:

- computer presentation programs
- multimedia programs
- computer-based training programs.

Again, the equipment required to support these materials must be included as part of the group.

Real items include both the models and the equipment needed for the learners to successfully engage in a learning activity. Models may demonstrate by means of cut-away sections the internal working of equipment. In most trade-related training real equipment is used as part of the learning activity.

MANAGING INSTRUCTIONAL MATERIALS

In an open learning setting the learners use the instructional material, rather than the teacher, who now facilitates the learners' interaction. In some learning environments learners are given copies of self-instruction booklets or they may be required to purchase their own. Textbooks that are only occasionally required by learners can be bought as class sets or the copies held by the teacher. A second option is to have the textbooks available in the library. When books or other resources are held by the teacher, borrowing procedures would need to be established in much the same way as a library. This is necessary for both security and availability of the resource.

Similar borrowing procedures would also need to be set up for other learning materials such as videotapes and computer programs. The only possible exception to this is when a teacher is closely supervising a group of learners in a classroom setting and materials do not have to be removed from the area.

Any equipment required to support the instructional materials must also be available to the learner. A regular maintenance schedule to ensure this availability should be set up. In most cases this type of equipment is accessible to learners to use in a central location and is not normally available for loan. However, the establishment of a booking system should be considered if the equipment is frequently used.

If learners are required to operate workshop equipment as part of their learning experience this must be done in a workshop environment. In this setting special consideration must be given to the safety of the learners to ensure their work is properly supervised. Particularly in trade related workshops it is important to closely supervise beginning learners to make sure safe working practices are followed all the time.

THE LEARNING RESOURCE CENTRE

In an open learning setting there are many resources that can be used, each of which must be managed and maintained. Therefore a learning resource centre should be in a centralized location where resources are stored and the learners can study. The establishment of such a centre will help solve many of the problems involved in managing materials and equipment. Any centre should be staffed with people responsible for both lending the learning materials and taking care of the equipment. A library is a learning resource centre. However, this need not be the only location. If you have a large number of learners, a number of smaller learning resource centres can be set up on a departmental basis. The advantage of this is that learners are now located closer to their classrooms and their teachers. And teachers, from the relevant subject areas, can be on duty to assist individual learners encountering learning difficulties.

SUPPORTING THE LEARNERS

An open learning setting is a new experience for many learners. Be prepared to offer as much support as possible to help learners overcome their initial fears.

For many learners, learning in an open setting is a new experience and they will often need support if they are to learn effectively. Even experienced learners will sometimes need support to ensure that they achieve the required objectives.

Effective learner support requires both facilities and learning materials. Learners need a proper place to study, and access to the appropriate equipment, workshops and laboratories. But these are the more obvious forms of support – learners also need support from their teachers.

When studying in an open learning environment the learners will need support in each of the following areas:

Before beginning the course

Learners will need to know:

Learners need support regarding how and what to study so make sure that you include that information in your learning material.

- what to study, what the content of the material is, and if they are relevant to their needs
- how to study and what study techniques to use. They will also need to know something about goal-setting and time-management.

During the course

While studying, learners might:

- have some problems with the content of the materials, no matter how well they are prepared
- have questions about assessment and need assistance preparing for the final assessment requirements
- have problems coping with stress, or have personal or study problems
- need support in relation to their jobs, if they are working, perhaps to arrange for time off for study purposes, to cope with various competing demands and to integrate their study with their work.

After the course

When the course is over, learners will need to know:

- what subjects they should study next
- the results of their efforts
- how they can improve in the future.

How these problems and concerns are dealt with will depend on the number of learners. A large number of learners may need:

- enrolment staff
- course advisors
- personal tutors
- subject tutors
- mentors
- self-help groups
- study skills counsellors.

A smaller group of learners may only need one teacher. But it must be recognized that learners will need some form of personal assistance with their study, no matter how well the materials were designed.

OPENING UP A CLOSED SETTING

Moving from a closed to a more open setting can be accomplished in many cases with a minimum of disruption to existing programmes of study.

Using existing resources

A simple method of opening up a closed setting is to develop or redevelop your lecture notes, handout material and other instructional material so that they are more 'user friendly' and allow for more individual study in your existing method of instruction. This can be accomplished through clearer writing, effective design and building in learner interaction.

If your current learning materials can be adapted rather than completely rewritten, you can use the same delivery strategy and allow other components of the materials to be completed individually or in small groups. Some work can be completed outside of class time when the learners can work at their own pace. Later your materials can be further adapted into a true open learning package. Your experience with the adapted learning material can be used as a form of field trial: the information and experience you gain will help you to redesign and produce an even more effective open learning package.

Sometimes it is quicker and easier to adapt existing materials than to start from scratch.

Adapting your learning materials

Whether you are writing or adapting existing material the same principles apply. The development of any learning package must be planned. Spending many hours writing learning material with little or no thought for the learners who are going to read and hopefully learn from it is not effective learning resource development.

'User friendly' learning materials should be prepared well in advance of when you will need them. When planning your materials keep the following points in mind:

- plan the overall structure of your materials first
- plan your materials so they do not overlap
- present the material in a logical sequence
- provide examples to explain your material
- ensure all objectives identified for the materials are covered
- plan all of your materials at the same time.

Writing the learning materials

Once you have determined how you are going to design and write your material you can start writing the actual body copy. When you are writing any learning material use the following as a guide to help ensure it is 'user friendly'.

- use a simple, informal style
- use personal pronouns such as 'I', 'you', or 'we'
- explain technical or unfamiliar words in the body of your text and define them in a glossary
- avoid clichés, slang and jargon
- use the minimum number of words
- be positive, eg 'Do this' is better than 'Don't do that'
- keep sentences and paragraphs short
- use simple words
- write in an active voice: 'this chapter is written in an active voice'.

Use lists and bullet points where possible but don't overdo it. For example:

Five devices that can aid learners are:

- summaries for each chapter

- subtext headings
- icons
- graphs
- table of contents.

This use of points is better than a text list such as: *Five devices which you can use to aid learners are summaries for each chapter, subtext headings, icons, graphs and a table of contents.*

One way you can check if your learning materials are written conversationally is to read them out aloud. This will help you to determine if the materials are tedious or awkward.

Access devices

Learning materials can be made more open if they are made more accessible to learners. Using so-called 'access devices' in learning material will make them more accessible. Access devices are things that help the reader find what they need, when they need it. Because people learn in many different ways, your learning materials should have a variety of access devices embedded in them. Objectives, advanced organizers, explanatory titles and headings are all examples of the different things that can be placed into learning materials as access devices.

Objectives, advanced organizers, explanation headers, titles and headings are all examples of advanced organizers. Make sure that you include as many as possible in your learning materials.

You can improve the design of your learning materials by using some or all of the following access devices:

- contents page
- visual signposts
- advanced organizers
- objectives
- introduction or overview
- headings

- concept maps
- diagrams and graphs
- marginal notes
- summaries
- glossary
- subject index.

Interactive devices

Learners will gain a great deal more from learning materials if they are actively involved in them. Simply reading the materials is not enough; you must build activities into them so that learners will become involved in the learning process.

Three simple ways to build interaction into your existing learning materials is through the use of:

- in-text questions
- concept maps
- summaries.

In-text questions

Include in-text questions in your materials every two or three pages to help learners check on their performance.

In-text questions are usually not assessed, but are provided to help the learner work more closely with the learning materials either during or after the learning event.

In-text questions can be used in two ways. First, learners complete the questions *after* the learning event. Second, you allow time during the learning event to complete the questions. If you use the second method you should correct the questions as part of your 'wrap-up' at the end of the learning event.

Concept map

A concept map is a useful way to outline learning materials as you present them (see Figure 1.3). Alternatively, to consolidate learning the learners could be asked to complete a concept map as a summary.

Summaries

Asking learners to summarize the content of a learning event will actively involve them in the learning process. You can assist the learners by giving them the major headings of what you will be covering during the learning event and asking them to complete the main points. If you simply give the learners a summary then all they will do is read the material.

PROJECTS AND ASSIGNMENTS

Projects help learners to apply skills and knowledge.

Projects and assignments are also an effective method of opening up a closed setting when used in conjunction with your existing learning materials. They allow the learners to work at their own pace and provide some choice of topics. Projects and/or assignments are usually given at the end of a unit of instruction and can be used for assessment purposes. Depending on the objectives of the unit the projects or assignments may be used as the main component of instruction.

Reading 1: Development and structure of an organization

The following reading will help you understand the considerations underlying the development and structuring of an organization.

This reading is the basis for the lecture that you will attend as part of this unit.

Exercise 1

When you have completed the reading please answer the following questions:

Q1. Why do organizations exist?

Q2. What is the difference between formal and informal organizations?

Q3. What are the factors affecting a manager's span of control?

Q4. What is the purpose of an organizational chart?

Write your answers to these questions on the following answer sheet. Answers can be found at the end of this book.

Figure 1.2 *Example of in-text questions*

A project helps guide the learners through some kind of investigation either on their own or in small groups. It usually involves the application of knowledge and skills to solve problems or complete specific tasks. The end product is usually a written report, a presentation or a model. Assignments are similar to projects but are usually set by the teacher. They generally take less time to complete than projects and tend to be set by the course leader, whereas learners are encouraged to choose their own project.

The aims of the project include:

● making the learners responsible for their own decisions
● developing creativity
● identifying and solving problems
● cooperating with others and teamworking

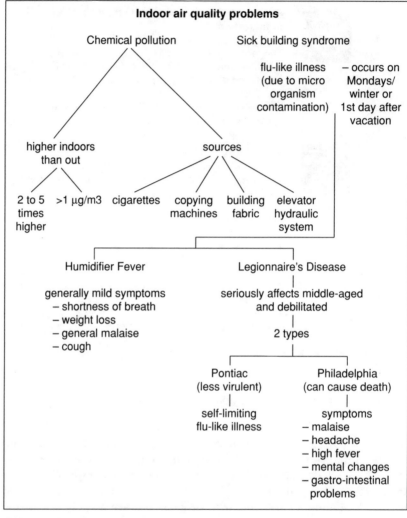

Figure 1.3 *Example of a concept map*

- developing written and oral skills
- developing goal-setting and time-management skills
- developing learners' practical knowledge of the subject
- developing resourcefulness
- developing appreciation for practical constraints
- developing negotiation skills.

The advantages to the teacher of project or assignment setting are that time is saved by not having to develop extensive learning materials. However, because projects and assignments are carried out individually, more personal supervision by the teacher may be required. This will mean the teacher to learner ratio has to be reduced.

You will need to structure a project or assignment for meaningful learning to occur. For example, you should:

- determine suitable subject matter
- set clear objectives
- develop an overview
- list the resources required
- sequence the suggested steps
- determine a timetable
- determine how it will be monitored
- determine how it will be assessed.

Write specific guidelines for your assignments and projects otherwise learners may only present you with descriptive information.

This method of structuring may seem to counter some of the aims of a project, but it does avoid problems, such as the learners not knowing where to start, taking too long on a project, or blaming others for failure.

The role of the teacher in a project or assignment can vary enormously. For example, the teacher can:

- teach research methods
- offer technical advice
- provide access to resources
- offer moral support
- monitor the project
- assist in planning the work.

Since the nature of projects or assignments can differ widely, the assessment criteria will need to be well-defined and explained in detail to the learners.

DIRECTED READING

Directed reading is a simple means of making your learning materials more open. Individualized learning materials often include reading assignments. However, the teacher may decide not to use them if these readings are:

- not at an appropriate level
- not totally relevant
- out of date
- expensive or scarce.

These problems can be overcome by giving learners a number of alternatives. This reduces the need for class sets of expensive resources. In a self-paced environment the learners learn at different rates and therefore will require the directed readings at different stages.

Additionally, you may need to:

- provide an introduction to the reading
- define new words or concepts in a glossary
- explain what areas of the reading may be out of date
- direct the learner to specific pages in a book
- develop a set of questions that the learner has to answer after they have completed the reading.

Directed reading is a simple method of allowing some form of self-pacing and choice in their study, but it must be planned and used appropriately.

LEARNING GUIDES

Consider developing learning guides as they are one of the most effective ways of individualizing existing learning materials.

Learning guides are an effective way of combining your existing learning material into an open learning package. A learning guide is generally a booklet that guides learners through a series of predetermined learning activities and directs them to a series of existing resources.

Figure 1.4 is an example of a page in a learning guide. In this example the learners are teachers learning how to develop a learning guide. The teachers are working individually and in a small group. First there is the reading which is an individual activity. Then there is the guided discussion on the extent of the learning guide. Finally there is the task of completing the learning guide specification form. This form is not shown in this example.

A typical learning guide informs the learner of the approximate time needed to complete the activity, the resources that should be used and the activity to be completed. It should include the following sections:

Learning Activities: Part One

Activity 1

The various activities described in part one of the learning guide should take about **3** hours to complete.

Read: Designing Learning Guides for TAFE and Industry: pp. 13 & 14
Workshop Package, Section 2: Where Do I Start?
Review: Learning Guide Specification Form.

Guided Discussion 1: Stating the problem
This activity introduces you to pro-formas (the Learning Guide Specification Form) to help you outline the overall extent of the learning guide being planned. In this exercise you will be expected to join in the guided discussion with ideas about how your document will be used in the course you are designing.

In groups of three to five persons and under the guidance of the course leader complete the following exercise.

Completing the Learning Guide Specification Form
Complete the Learning Guide Specification using your own course materials as a guide and adding additional notes where necessary.

Figure 1.4   *An example of an activity sheet*

- title page
- contents page
- directions for use
- learning objectives
- required knowledge and skills
- various learning activities and resources
- various self-assessment activities
- glossary
- selected references.

CONCLUSION

This chapter has described various ways in which you can open up a closed setting. The method you choose, of course, will depend on your teaching learning environment. There are a number of relatively simple ways of opening up a closed system, and many of the problems of creating an open learning setting can be solved by careful resource management, supporting the learners and designing effective instructional materials.

Chapter 2

Doing Something Different in the Classroom: Making Delivery Work for You

SUMMARY

You are prepared to deliver the new course or learning materials – but what about your learners? This chapter discusses aspects of dealing with learner expectation during the delivery stage. One important aspect is assuring everybody in the community of the learner that the new course and materials are appropriate to the education and training purpose.

INTRODUCTION

The discussions and examples in this chapter deal with two situations:

1. You might be delivering a course and materials you have developed yourself.
2. In today's world of education and training there is a move towards national curriculum documents or courses. Therefore, you could be delivering a course, probably with minimal support, that has been developed by someone else.

In both settings there are implications for teachers at both implementation and delivery of the new course and the course materials.

In this chapter the focus is on the learners' expectations of new courses or course materials. The contextual setting is how you can make the delivery work for you and the learners.

For the purpose of this chapter, the term 'learner' has been divided into preschool and secondary learners, older learners and learners who are more independent. This is to recognize that delivery using new or different techniques and methods, or new courses, may raise differing sets of issues and concerns for learners and for the community of the learners. There are different considerations for learners in the training setting.

This chapter examines these issues and concludes with a discussion of the shift towards learners taking a greater role in and responsibility for their learning. The chapter discusses the implications for everyone involved in the ongoing process of the course and for course materials planning, development, delivery and evaluation.

The first three parts of the chapter deal with young learners, older learners and independent learners. The final part outlines how you can make the delivery of learning materials work for both you and the learners.

NEW MATERIALS OR COURSES AND YOUNG LEARNERS

The education of your learners may not feature frequently in the media as a political issue. The influence on the learner of the 'formal' education and training system and the influence of the 'home' on the learners' development will be a continual source of argument. Although it would be a sweeping generalization to claim that in the past, parents and caregivers have not been interested in the education of their young, it is true that today's parents and caregivers are more involved in the education of their charges. Parents and caregivers are showing an increasing concern for education as a grounding for further education and a place in the socio-economic world of work – they want to give young people a good start on their career path.

This influence of the home gives rise to an issue that rests not so much with the learners but with the parents or caregivers. What happens to your course or materials if those parents or caregivers are not followers of the shifts in education?

Example 1

The history of innovation in education is full of well-intended courses or materials running into criticism, controversy and failure. The introduction of sex education courses is a familiar case. However, even in traditional subjects such as English and maths, public debate and suspicion within establishments have impeded new teaching ideas.

Example 2

Parents and caregivers often have their own memory of school. A new programme for younger learners could bring about protest from those remembering their own education; they may compare their experiences with this 'new stuff', and, as it is not the way they did it, parents and caregivers could assert that the new stuff is inferior.

If the planning and development stages have included the distribution to the community of information about the changes, the possibility of protests of this kind will be reduced, and hopefully for you, could be avoided altogether.

There is a second issue that relates to the people (parents, caregivers, peers and siblings – the community of the learner) who surround young learners and their expectations during learning. Often young learners have been told what to expect at school; this is usually based on their parents' or caregivers' experience of school. And that experience is often very out of date. Sometimes older siblings take pleasure in recounting stories (both real and made up) about their experiences in a course or with a particular teacher.

An interesting side issue (if you have the time) might be to consider how to 'demystify' the influence of this community on the learners' perception of 'going to school', a 'new' course or subject, or new course and materials.

During the delivery process it will pay you and members of the team to monitor the initial responses to the course and materials. This feedback is necessary for evaluating the materials or course; it will assist you in recognizing possible problem areas; and it will assist you in determining if the outcomes of the new course and materials will be achieved. To do this you will need to record the observations of the teachers, the responses of the learners and any 'incidents' that occur. These could provide informing evidence in the evaluation of the course and materials.

Two small reminders on young people and learning

It is obviously nonsense to contend that young people entering education have no prior learning experience. Those with the physical capabilities have learned to talk, many are able to recognize words and some are able to translate word patterns as reading. They will have progressed from uncoordinated infants to young persons with varying degrees of hand-eye manipulation skills. Many will have a wisdom that is older than their years – with a refreshing simplicity that shows the world-weary concepts of adults in a poor light.

In reality, the learner entering the formal school system for the first time brings with them three to six years of collecting information to help them to cope with the real world. Do we still treat them as if they are naive? The following questions reinforce the points to think about.

- How do teachers cope with individual differences among young learners?
- How are the young learners going to respond to a new course or course materials different to those that their parents or caregivers and older siblings have experienced, and have described in vivid detail? The young learner is faced with a dilemma. Who do they believe: their 'family' or the 'teacher'?

A different dilemma arises with the older learner.

NEW MATERIALS OR COURSES AND OLDER LEARNERS

This part of the chapter discusses some of the implications for older learners when new courses and materials are brought into their teaching and learning.

It is too easy to assume that *older* learners are *experienced* learners with a wide variety of learning skills. Remember that many learners may have had little variation in their 'learning diet', including the learning strategies, since the learner entered the formal education system.

What happens when course content changes or a new course is introduced? In the table opposite, the effect on the learners changes from the position before the introduction to learning (no effect) to the third cohort position (acceptance of the course as the 'norm').

Around the time of the introduction of a new course it is possible that learners may experience some sense of dislocation and disruption. It is up to you to see that the introduction of the new course and materials is as smooth as possible.

A question that needs to be asked is whether there is a flow-on effect? Table 2.1 attempts to illustrate the problem. Trying to state the problem clearly: Last year's learners did the 'old' course, this year's

Table 2.1   *The effect on learners of changes in course content*

	Year before introduction	First year of new course	Second cohort of new course	Third cohort of new course
Effect on learner	Nil, because the learner is still undertaking the old course	Depends on the learner's expectatations	Depends on what the learner entering the course has heard	By this time most learners will accept the course as the 'norm'
Outcomes for learners	No, or limited, knowledge of change	Knowledge of change. May or may not accept the change	Knowledge of change. More willing to accept the change	The course is the 'norm'
Revision		Probably happening as the course and materials are being developed		

learners are doing the 'new' course; should we be concerned that last year's learners may be disadvantaged by not having had full experience of the new course? How do we try and redress a possibility of the learners in the 'old' course not being up to date?

Then there is the problem of the expected and predictable. Older learners are experienced in certain patterns of learning and different organizational settings, such as the use of one classroom and one teacher in 'primary' education. The general mayhem of moving classrooms as the timetable dictates occurs in the 'secondary' or junior-high years. Then there is the 'here is the timetable, make it work for you' of college and university. What many learners at all levels are not expecting is a change in the way courses are delivered or the demands this may place on them. These new courses or materials for older learners could be seen as a threat because they challenge their perception of education. The task that faces you is to make the new course and materials non-threatening.

There will be other learners who may feel threatened because of prior experience of new courses or materials. If their previous experience is negative they will think 'why me'? and approach it in a way that causes them least anxiety and involvement. If you are aware of this situation perhaps there is something in the delivery strategy to make these new materials less of a threat to the learner.

There are three other expectations the older learner may have, rightly or wrongly. For some learners, and for some traditionalists in the community of the learner, the first expectation can be put simply: the teacher is the expert and should be telling the learners what to do. This is known variously as the 'transmitter of cultural heritage' or 'filling the empty vessel'. These learners expect to be told and then examined. The people who populate the community of the learner will expect this type of instruction for learners. Any other form of 'learning' is seen by these people as a soft option at best, and non-educational.

As a person involved in the delivery of educational and training courses and materials, you may have to develop strategies to overcome the perception that new courses and materials are not soft options.

Another expectation of both learners and the community of learners is that teachers, learners and their community are involved in the same learning process. This could be seen as 'learning the socialization'. At the 'end' of the learning process the learner will be a functioning member of the community. The assumption that there is an 'end' is denied by the philosophy that is now dominant of life-long learning, and leads to the third possibility.

The third expectation is that learners will be supported by the educational community to develop their view of the world and the skills the learner requires for their ongoing learning capabilities. These expectations seem to ignore several factors about the process of education and training.

First, the process of education and training is full of selection of content. This selection currently is based on the teacher's experience. As a result, the material used is generally idiosyncratic. This, in part, explains why two teachers will rarely handle the same content in exactly the same manner. However, this situation is changing in many countries as the development of 'standards' and 'competencies' in education and training is being adopted. It should be added that even the publication of standards and competencies is frustrated by the human element of the teacher. And learners do not progress on a continuum in a smooth manner.

The second factor that could give rise to the concerns for older learners is when new courses and materials suggest that the education and training are offered as life-long learning. This is in conflict with the 'old' view that at the end of education and training there was a job for life. Today, education addresses the need for continual training and development in view of changes in workplace practices and new technology. This means that initial education and training must prepare people for life-long education and training. There is also an underlying recognition that today, and in the future, changes in workplace practices could be more rapid. This will require even faster responses to education and training needs by those in the workplace.

A third factor is that until recently the ability of learners to determine their learning needs has not been considered in most traditional education and training settings. However, a more informed view of learners having an input into their learning and training requirements indicates that, given an open and flexible option to course enrolment and course completion, learners will more successfully complete courses at the required standard under conditions that they negotiate, than they will in a traditional rigid (time serving) course.

NEW MATERIALS OR COURSES AND INDEPENDENT LEARNERS

In this part of the chapter the independent learner is discussed.

In order to make delivery work for you with independent learners it's a good idea to re-examine the assumptions on which the course and materials were developed. As a general rule, more experienced learners bring with them a variety of stances based on influences in their prior learning. These influences could be related to the distinction between compulsory education (usually to a specific age level), non-compulsory education and voluntary education and training.

Compulsory education and training

As a generalization, many independent learners may not be enthusiastic about returning to compulsory education and training. At its worst, compulsory education and training for these learners can generate negative emotions if they find the experience irrelevant, condescending or interfering with a life outside the institution or their needs.

However, if the compulsory education or training is an area that is relevant to them, such as changes in workplace practices or as a result of the impact of technology, the response of independent learners may be different. Appropriate consultation about times and means of delivery could mean that the individual needs of these independent learners can be considered.

This is possible for the following reasons:

- these learners are mature and generally more articulate
- the existing skills and abilities of these learners are needed in their workplace
- these learners recognize their need for new skills and knowledge.

What results in this setting is negotiated workplace training that benefits both the employer, employee and the productivity of the company.

Non-compulsory education and independent learners

Remember that in adult and further education many people enrol in courses and complete only those parts that are of immediate benefit to them, so plan accordingly!

For delivering of new courses and materials the use of non-compulsory education is considered to benefit learners because they only need attend if the education and training is relevant. Thus, possible problems or complaints based on the learner's perception of repeating already known material could be reduced.

However, one drawback is that this use of non-compulsory education and training can lead to haphazard attendance. This gives rise to problems of continuity in a particular learner's education and the administration of traditional concepts of attendance, which can lead to problems for the teachers in constant monitoring of learner progress and frustration in the learner. We are aware of this at both college and university level where lectures may not be compulsory.

Recognizing the independent learner within the new framework

One possible path for the independent learner is to gain recognition for not only the formally or certified skills they hold but for the skills gained as part of their life. It may be possible to recognize such informally gained skills or knowledge towards credits, exemptions, or progression within the course. Exemptions could reduce the frustration of repeating the known and the time-serving nature of traditional courses. There will, however, need to be an administrative infrastructure to do this, but the outcome could only serve to increase the enthusiasm of the independent learner.

Voluntary education and independent learners

Voluntary education and training has two aspects. The first is the desire of the independent learner to gain information and skills. The second is the offer by employers and training agencies to staff and the community to participate in training. These courses, generally short in time, involve skills training or updating. For learners or participants in these courses attendance may not be totally voluntary, particularly if the aim of the course is to maintain or gain employment skills. However, the independent learner has the choice to update their knowledge and skills.

With independent learners there needs to be a realistic approach to the task of delivering education and training through the use of appropriate methodologies in an understood setting.

WHY MAKE THE SIMPLE COMPLEX?

Returning to the general theme of making delivery work for you, avoid complicating learning unnecessarily.

An illustration of the dangers of overcomplication has been the use of expensive high technology as electronic page turners. In these cases the delivery of new courses and the use of new materials have been developed with focus on the technology rather than the course content. This causes the learner to be working with activities requiring higher-order skills, sometimes before the basic material had been covered. As a consequence, materials for these courses, which should be simple to produce, are replaced with expensive technology.

Sometimes technology is used in the mistaken belief that working with exciting new equipment will engender more enthusiasm in the learner. In some cases all it does is increase the frustration in both the teacher and the learner when adequate or inappropriate material causes the learning activity to be only a partial success.

The bottom line is making the delivery of the course and materials work for you and the learner.

LEARNING HOW TO LEARN

There is a growing recognition of a conflict between teaching content and the learner developing the skills needed to take charge of their own learning. If teaching content is your concern, you might claim that you are already teaching *how* to learn. But, there is now a 'new' education and training area – 'learning how to learn'.

Subject content needs to be known, and it is recognized that there are skills that need to be acquired. But this should be seen against a background of information explosion, changes in the world, the influence of technology of the way many jobs are being performed (or are disappearing), and a future where it is increasingly difficult to make long-term predictions about employment opportunities. In this setting, the phrase 'life-long learning' has gained some significance. That life has always been a learning experience is a fact that is sometimes conveniently forgotten. However, life-long learning indicates a significant shift in the education and training agenda. This shift could be the cause of new courses and materials.

In the previous sections on learners several points were made about the organization of delivery. These include for young learners:

● How do teachers cope with individual difference among young learners when delivering new courses and materials?
● Who do young learners believe – their 'family' or the 'teacher' – when faced with conflicting versions of 'What they should do at school'?

Then there are the considerations for older learners:

● Do we try to redress a possibility of the learners in the 'old' course not being brought up to date?
● What are the strategies to overcome the perception that new courses and materials are soft options?

It may seem simplistic, but the principal aim is to make learners independent. Learners should become competent in the knowledge, skills and attitudes delivered in the course and course materials. This should lead to a transition from learner to a practitioner with increased skills and abilities.

What is a practitioner?

As a rule of thumb, a practitioner is a person who can perform a specified task to an expected level on a consistent basis. The main problem with that definition is that it lacks conditions of performance and outcomes.

A more useful definition would include the conditions of acceptable performance at any of the three general levels of learner discussed in this chapter. In part these involve the ability demonstrated in a variety of educational and training settings, showing the personal development of the learner. For example:

- For the young learner development might be demonstrated by the ability to add up several sets of numbers.
- For the older learner this may be demonstrated by the ability to determine a course of action to follow in order to gain information and offer a possible solution to a problem.
- For the independent learner, their choice to attend a course and self-expectation indicates that they are approaching the level of a practitioner. They already have knowledge and expertise and are seeking to join other experts.

At each level the learner is being asked to perform tasks at a level appropriate to expected performance and as a practitioner with that level of 'expertise'.

Making the delivery work for you

In the best of all worlds, when you come to deliver a course, both the course and the materials should already be working for you. The learners and the community of learners should have some idea of the work in store for them. But they can be daunting – you are asking them to face a future of which they have no knowledge, and little comprehension of the possible outcomes. Some learners could feel a sense of apprehension or real threat. It is your task, and that of any support people, to answer questions, allay fears and remain positive about the new course and materials.

In theory, this should be an easy task because you have all the information you need. In reality, it can be frustrating, as many of the same questions will arise in different settings and contexts. You will have to control your sense of frustration that you already have answered these queries.

One strategy you might try is to re-issue the documentation to learners, showing the consultation process that gave rise to the new course and materials. You have to reassure the community of the learner. It may be that not all the documentation is needed, only key parts of it. This should serve to 'jog' memories of the consultation process and the role of the players in the process. Another strategy for use with the learners, during the delivery process, is to provide them with feedback on their abilities to cope with the course and materials.

CONCLUSION

In this chapter issues involved in making the delivery process work for you have been discussed. It is recognized that different courses and materials could give rise to different issues of delivery. It is also recognized that making delivery work adds to the workload. However, is strategies are considered at the delivery stage, later administrative difficulties for you and any anxiety in the learners, can be reduced. You will have to make the decision about how best you can make the process work for you.

Chapter 3
Coping with Newness

SUMMARY

Here and elsewhere in this book we talk about the educational community in which you operate. The community involves everyone in the education and training process. These members may be considered stakeholders. At any one time, there will be different levels of interest shown by people in the educational community. At some points the new course and materials may be of concern to only particular stakeholders. You need to recognize that planning, development and delivery of a new course or course materials development and delivery of a new course or course materials is a learning process process for some of these stakeholders. In this chapter we address some of the concerns stakeholders may raise from their perspective.

INTRODUCTION

How do we cope when faced with something new? Some people embrace it with a will, others take a more reserved approach. If you are faced with the task of delivery or implementation of a course and materials, what concerns might be raised by stakeholders?

In this chapter, stakeholders are those with a clearly defined role or concern in the education and training process. It will be that some stakeholders are only concerned with part of the process, while other stakeholders are involved in every aspect of the process.

This chapter is broken into the following sections:

- supporters and antagonists
- managing change at the delivery stage
- gathering information at delivery
- tracking the process of the implementation
- gathering evidence for evaluation.

The people who make up your educational community will rarely be alike. They will come from different backgrounds, perhaps different levels of education and will remember their education in different ways. Therefore it is highly probable that there will be a variety of reactions from people to the proposed change. Some will embrace the changes with enthusiasm, or you might find yourself coping with those who view the new and unusual with antagonism.

SUPPORTERS AND ANTAGONISTS

Supporters of change

Be wary of those who support you. Not because their support may be superficial, or because they are waiting for you to fail. The main reason to be wary of supporters is that they may be too enthusiastic. You may have convinced them of the need for change and suddenly they believe the rest of the world also supports the idea. Not only could they go off at express train speed but they could also go off the rails. In their enthusiasm they may expect actions or activities not envisioned in the course or materials, and may seek to extend the course of action beyond the mandate without understanding the practical constraints. Eventually, when either you, or other members of the community involved in the project, calm down these enthusiasts, they may become disillusioned and perhaps even resentful that their good intentions and positive outlook were not appreciated. It may be difficult to identify these people in the overall design and development process. However, you need to be aware of the possibility of these people 'surfacing' at some stage in the project. Handled diplomatically these people may be content to see their ideas held over to a further stage of the project. Under no circumstances should you attempt to avoid these people by claiming there is a higher authority and the matter is out of your hands. It may be that these people approach that authority and the process does end up out of your hands.

Antagonists to change

The energy and enthusiasm that is often generated by new course or materials development activities can be a source of jealousy for others. This jealousy can lead to problems at the delivery stage. It may be in the form of criticizing the course or materials even before they are at the deliverable stage. This can lead to an erosion of confidence in the course or materials before delivery, and will magnify even minor problems that might arise. The main reasons for this negative reaction are not hard to recognize. It may have to do with budget allocation: any course development and course materials development project is going to attract funding. In times of tight economic constraints on education and training budgets, it is likely that there have to be trade-offs between funding existing programmes and funding new programmes and materials. It is therefore likely that people facing possible funding cuts will question, and maybe call into doubt, the need for new courses and materials.

At the point of delivery of the new course and materials you will need to reassess the support you have for the initiative.

Another reason people oppose change is fear of the new. This is natural as change requires people to operate in ways that are unfamiliar and the worry of failure to cope in these new surroundings is to be expected. This fear can be compounded if it is combined with previous experience. People who have been through unsuccessful innovation and change may have a jaundiced view. These people may have been involved in change without full or adequate consultation; often the attempt at change has been short-lived. This happens particularly when a so-called 'hot shot' enters the scene, makes changes and then moves on without ensuring that there is adequate support to enable the changes to be maintained.

Change for the sake of change

In many education and training systems around the world there have been changes in structures, systems and philosophies. A main feature of these changes seems to be that change itself is the goal. If this change were to result in constantly improving the level of education and training that would be fine. But many of the restructures seem to do with administration, and changes in education and training have occurred because of structural and systematic changes. In reality, education and training have continued while the administrative structures and systems have been rearranged. While many of these changes have seemed cosmetic, there have been some real and beneficial changes in education and training, such as the move towards competency based curricula.

As you deliver your course material(s) remember that change is inevitable and you will have to respond to that change in one way or another.

Enforced change

There are two other factors that need to be considered in the change process. The first is the information technology revolution; the second is the shift in education and training from education for a job to life-long education and training. In other words, just to keep up with developments in the world, everyone needs to be constantly monitoring and updating their skills and knowledge as change impinges on them and the jobs they do. In part, this second shift is given false emphasis, in that throughout history people have had to adapt to change in their employment. But it is true that today these changes are happening faster as new technology impacts on work skills.

However, a major problem is that the community may not be informed of the ramifications to education and training and employment prospects. There is also the possibility that the learners are not informed of alternatives to the traditional concepts of being an employee.

In many countries there is a change in work practices caused by new technologies. The move towards competency based education and training incorporating core and specialist competencies is but one indicator of the move towards lifelong learning to cope with the world of change rather than a fixed world. Competency-based learning is also an indicator that learners need to develop a sense of purpose in their education and training, which has little to do with the traditional organization of 'teaching'. However, the wider community involved in education may not be aware of the changes and need to be informed now. If they are not given this information, there will be a continual need to argue the reason for change within the community of the learner.

Informing the community about change

Many of the parents and caregivers out there in the world beyond the educational institution still consider that their offspring or charges should be taught in the same way they were. Many of these adults have not picked up on lifelong learning. Why should they? Yet these same people are lifelong learners in that they have adapted to changing situations in employment and learned the skills to remain in or gain employment. The problem is that these people are not able to recognize their own adaptive skills. It should be a function of education and training institutions to make clear that ongoing change will be the norm and that learners are able to adapt.

Support will also be withheld if members of the community deem that new methods of learning are experiments. For these people, 'experiment' implies that the course and materials are not proven and could threaten their child's ability to compete in the real world. This may cause resistance to your programme.

The in-built problem with change and change strategies is that you are dealing with individuals, and their response to the challenges of change will be idiosyncratic. The responses of parents and caregivers to a new methodology or project have been mentioned. You must also consider the response of the learners who are unaware that they are being involved in a new programme.

One final factor in the level of support has to do with the mythology of schooling as an embedded or traditional expectation. How does your new course confront traditional expectations? Has any possible conflict been discussed with the educational community?

MANAGING CHANGE AT THE DELIVERY STAGE

Change in education and training courses is not an exact process. In part, this is because people are involved. In the education and training world the wish by someone to instigate change must survive the scrutiny of the people who will be affected by the change.

Change is a people process so make sure that all the right people are involved.

As a people process, and at the delivery stage, you will need to make sure that the following processes are managed.

First, the course and materials must be sanctioned and the wider community informed. Sanctioning will consist of all the actions undertaken in planning and preparing the course and materials. This will include course documentation, resource appraisal, development of course materials and consultation with the community of the learner. In particular, it will involve the approval of the course documents by the stakeholders as representatives of the educational and training community.

When the delivery stage is reached, the following processes and issues will need to be revisited.

Process 1: organization of timetables

In any teaching or training institution utilization of the time available to learners is a serious consideration. In schools' timetables this is seen in the ongoing tension between the allocation of time to humanities/arts and to science/technology. In post-school institutions the tension can be generated by the student ratios and the mix of lectures, tutorials and practical sessions.

A real problem with timetables is that they seem to be driven by resource availability; the rooms and teachers. A further timetable issue could arise from the demand for time that your new course places on the students.

Consider the case of an undergraduate course in drama. The information sessions and the workshops could be handled in the timetable, but the extra time taken for rehearsals for a production and the performances caused students to skip classes in other subjects. This had some effect on their results, and it angered teaching staff in other subjects when any of these students turned up to find out what they had missed in the classes they skipped. This is not good for the educational community.

Remember that a place in the timetable may have some history behind it. If your course is seen to threaten that 'order' then you will meet with some opposition to the change, unless you have a strategy to placate those threatened. Hopefully you have taken this into account during the systematic planning of the course. If not, you will need to recognize 'timetable' as an issue and work with colleagues to resolve difficulties. The same general advice holds for overcoming resistance because of threats to space or room allocation if these have not been worked through in the planning stages.

Process 2: organization of teaching spaces

When setting up a new course you may want to use the spaces available in a different way. If this is planned for, then 'room owners', and the power brokers of space utilization such as janitors, cleaners, etc, will have been informed. If they are happy, then some of the problems associated with teaching spaces will not arise.

However, when you are at the delivery stage there is still the potential for teaching space problems to occur. Remember that up to the delivery stage the new course and materials have been very much a paper based exercise. The calls on resources of space and time (not to mention money) have been subjects in meetings and drafting documents. Now, at delivery of the new course and materials, the real calls on space, time and money are about to happen.

Process 3: different layout of teaching space

If you are fortunate, you may have a 'dedicated space' available to you for the single purpose of delivery of the new course and materials.

That's fine, but beware of creating jealousy. If this space previously belonged to somebody else and you have displaced them, there is a possibility of tension between you and that person. At worst, this can cause real friction, and resentment of you, the programme and the materials.

In many situations the space you use will be shared with others, and you do not have a dedicated space to present the new course or materials. Others will use this space and change it to meet their needs as a teaching and learning area. It is easy to suggest that the solution is to discuss and compromise. The difficulty is that more often than not the result of compromise is a no-win situation for all. The ability to negotiate a win situation for all is rare – but that does not mean that the win situation for all is not attainable. Goodwill is essential, and one of the starting points is to recognize the dilemma and consult on possible compromises. These can range from the real need to rearrange furniture to the responsibility to restore the room to a 'reasonable' state for use by others.

The need for security of special equipment should have been recognized and dealt with in the planning stage. Security is an issue in all learning spaces, but it is even more of an issue if the space is shared with others.

Will the delivery of your course and the new materials cause disturbance to those in surrounding teaching areas? This question is asked because you may have to deal with complaints, some of which could have been seen at the planning or development stages – or could they?

In summary, these are local issues, involving certain members of the community of the learners, in the management of the delivery of a new course and materials. It is to be hoped that these issues were addressed at the planning and development stage. If not, they need to be addressed immediately.

GATHERING INFORMATION AT DELIVERY

During the delivery of the new course and materials you could be referring back to the information gathered from the community about the course and documented in the planning and preparation stage. The need to do so may be infrequent. However, at the delivery stage you should expect questions from those involved in the delivery process and this could have you referring back to earlier decisions. While the need for clarification could become a nuisance, you will have to answer the queries. The positive side is that if these questions are recorded, using something like a diary, they will provide useful information on the course, the course term, or the management of the process of course delivery. This record will be valuable for later reporting on the course and materials.

The second part of the information gathering exercise is to keep the community informed. In a case such as simple changes to materials in a classroom, this reporting back need not be complex, but it must be systematic. In some settings it could amount to informing the community that the use of the new materials has started, with a progress report at a later date. And at an even later date you may report on the outcome.

Although systematic, such a simple process may be inappropriate in other settings. If the new course and materials are more complex or have a higher profile, you may need to refer back to the community more comprehensively. In particular, you will need to gather information to support an evaluation of the new course and materials for the community of the learners.

As a final point, the need to gather information enables you to report back to the educational and training community. From this reporting process you might well expect members of the community to raise questions about the process and the outcomes for the learners. However, by referring back to the community you are reassuring them of their role in the education and training process and ensuring their continuing support.

Gathering of information will also be of use in the evaluation process.

TRACKING THE PROCESS

The mechanisms for tracking new course and materials implementation and delivery should have been developed at the planning and development stage.

The need to track the process is to determine if there are areas for improvement, it is a quality issue. Simply put, tracking the process the first time through will give useful feedback. Importantly, feedback provides indicators that could become benchmarks. These benchmarks will serve as reference points for subsequent deliveries of the course or use of the materials.

Tracking the process is also important if there is a team involved in the course delivery or the materials are being delivered in different locations. In these cases it will be important to collect and collate the responses of the learners and the teachers, and their reactions to the use of the course and materials. Both learner and teacher responses are essential for evaluation.

GATHERING EVIDENCE FOR EVALUATION

While the mechanisms for gathering information as evidence for an evaluation of the course and materials should have been handled at the planning and development stage, it is during the delivery stage that the information is collected. In the fourth book in this series, *Evaluating a Course*, the issues of evaluation are discussed.

Briefly, there are three types of information that could and should be collected:

- qualitative
- – validated test items undertaken by the learner
- – marks or results
- quantitative
- – scores developed from assessment tasks set for analysis, evaluation and reporting
- anecdotal
- – information, such as spontaneous comments offered by learners using the course and materials, offers insight into the information collected by qualitative and quantitative means.

DELIVERY OF INTERNET BASED MATERIALS

In this chapter the relationship of the teacher and the differing role of teachers to adults and teachers to younger learners have been considered. The different perspectives held by the current population of learners as to the change in the learning environment are not so much to do with doing something different in the classroom as to being in a different classroom. In this section of the chapter the following topics will be discussed in relation to using the Internet.

- coping with the newness
- adults
- the Internet is new
- young learners
- the Internet is now

- delivery of on-line learning materials
- the Intranet as a tool

The use of the Internet as a delivery tool needs to be seen in relation to the Internet itself. The Internet provides access to a huge range of information. As such, it breaks down the subject matter expertise traditionally associated with teachers and teaching in institutions. A computer connected to the Internet in the library or a classroom expands the options for access to resources beyond those physically available on site.

For a learner with access to a computer in the home or workplace or a cybercafe as a course deliverer you must take into account that the learner has access to information of their interest beyond what you are capable of offering at your course delivery site.

A learner accessing a course over the Internet has access to a vast amount of information. The information that is collected may be eclectic or even perverse. The challenge for the learner is to make the information meaningful. The challenge for the person delivering the course is to accept as valid or argue the inappropriateness of this information in relation to the expected outcomes of the course. This also has implications for the learners and their capacity to cope in a new setting.

Coping with the newness

For the world the Internet is new. However, it is a fallacy to assert that adults are not assimilators of new technology. Most airport lounges are full of people using mobile phones and laptop computers. In other settings people use Automatic Teller Machines, word processing and spread sheet applications on computers on a regular basis.

There is a perception among the image-makers that the Internet is now and is for young people. It is a truism to assert that young people are early assimilators of the use of new technologies. Yet one only has to do an Internet search to see that information providers on the Internet range from proud parents announcing a birth to newly formed rock bands announcing concert dates.

Among all this information is material about careers, courses, general knowledge, skills forming information and histories and futures.

There is an expectation that adult users of the Internet are able to control their Internet working. There is a suspicion that many young people without the skills to develop sophisticated use of the Internet waste time in tangential searches. Anecdotal information suggests that for many users of the Internet the ability to construct meaningful searches is limited. As the research literature on the user's ability to construct searches to support education and training is minimal, this suggests an avenue for further research.

Delivery of Internet based materials

There are course materials on the Internet now. And it is possible to enrol, participate, gain credits and graduate electronically, but many of the courses deal with how to develop a web site on the Internet. It appears that at least one issue has been lost in the use of technology for course delivery. And this is not the first time.

The use of radio, film, television and satellite in general have seen technology as a tail wagging the educational dog. One example that is exempt is the use of 'School of the Air' low cost radio technology in Australia. The use of radio communication for teaching in Australia was a consequence of the establishment of a radio communications network to support the provision of medical services to people in remote locations. The ability for rapid response through radio requests for help and service provided by aircraft was recognized in Australia prior to World War Two. What became apparent soon after the establishment of the service was the potential for communication at other than emergency levels. The service soon took on an educational perspective.

The initial technology of the wireless has given way to current technologies of the satellite phone. However, the context is the same. The context is of delivering education and training to people via the use of the most appropriate technology. I have some reservations about the use of technology to deliver courses via the Internet, however.

A criticism that I would have of some of these courses is that they are essentially computer based versions of courses delivered in a face-to-face mode or by text based distance education. In these cases the Internet serves as a technological barrier to course delivery, in that it requires specific equipment to access the information. This may not be a problem in some settings. However, the most effective aspects for people involved in developing course material for use on the Internet is to resolve the relationship between the delivery aspects required for information transfer of the content and the appropriate uses of the attributes of the Internet.

The Intranet as a tool

While it is fashionable to write in terms of the wide area distribution of course information and learning materials offered by the Internet, some forget the possibility of offering course information and, more particularly, course content and activities on an Intranet. As a general rule an Intranet is defined as a company or institution wide network providing information channels via computer applications.

The Intranet as a tool has many uses. Primarily it can become a source of corporate knowledge by being the means of internal communication. The move towards a paperless office is still a myth. The use of an Intranet has the potential to reduce missed telephone calls and reduce the paper flow created by the intra office memo.

CONCLUSION

The education and training process attracts the interest of particular groups within the community at different times. Community members are stakeholders, and it is important to recognize that the process of planning, development and delivery of a new course and materials might be a learning process for some of these stakeholders.

Stakeholders will also have their own agenda; you will need to take into account different needs and expectations within the community.

Remember:

- be wary of over enthusiastic supporters – they could get carried away.
- be prepared for antagonism caused by jealousy, fear of the unknown and competition.
- include the community of the learner in the management of the delivery of a new course and materials – this should be incorporated at the planning and development stage.
- be aware that changes in the world, such as the information technology revolution, have an impact on types of education and training, and course delivery.

The shift in education and training from education for a job, to lifelong education and training affects the learner and community expectations.

You are dealing with people whose responses to the challenges of new courses and materials will be idiosyncratic. Some will embrace the new with enthusiasm, others will view changes with antagonism. Hopefully the consultation that took place as part of the planning and preparation process will have alerted community members or stakeholders to the change, and will have alerted you to the likely reactions. However, throughout delivery of the new course and materials you may still have to 'educate' some members of the educational and training community.

Chapter 4
Expecting the Unexpected

SUMMARY
Everything is ready for delivery of the course. The plan is set; the support materials for the learners are ready. You have anticipated potential problems for the delivery of a new course and materials, and you may believe every eventuality is covered. However, if there is a lingering doubt that something has been missed, listen to the doubt.

INTRODUCTION

Preparing for the unexpected is fundamental to good implementations and delivery strategy. The previous two chapters discussed coping with the new on the part of the people taking part and the learners. This chapter addresses unexpected problems that could arise during delivery. Some are minor; others could be catastrophic for the acceptance of the new course or materials. For example, if you have had experience with technology such as computers or videotapes, you will know that the computer 'going down' just when you need it, or the heads on the video replay machine becoming clogged, are to be expected. These things are sent to try the patience of us all. However, it does pay to consider exactly these eventualities and to have plan to cover them.

Erratic technology is not the only danger for effective delivery. The unexpected response of learners when they get their hands on the materials have been discussed in the previous two chapters. But what about changes in the level of support? While it may never happen to you, just consider what you might do if changes in the level of support for your initiative arise from a change in

- government
- government funding
- community support.

WHAT HAPPENS IF THERE IS A CHANGE IN GOVERNMENT?

It is difficult to map out a possible course of action when there is a change in government. It is even more difficult to provide advice when there is a change of educational philosophy brought about by a change of government. Currently in the world of educational philosophy there are theoretical approaches such as behavourism, humanism and constructionism. While it may be difficult to reconcile these philosophical stances in an educational context, what are the means to reconcile them in a changing political context? The new course and materials you are about to deliver may not be seen as fitting into the educational philosophy of the new government. If this is the case, the new course and materials may be under threat; but if the documentation for the course and materials is supportable the threat is reduced. After all, people believe that their prosperity is linked to education and training: it enables them to develop their economic well-being and contribute to the development of the community. The bottom line is that programmes can be stopped when there is a change of government, if the course or course materials do not fit in with the incoming government's educational philosophy. Equally, governments can change funding support through a change in their determined priorities.

WHAT HAPPENS IF THERE IS A CHANGE IN FUNDING?

Changes in government policy are not always predictable. For example, at the moment support is weighted towards technological solutions to education and training problems arising because of the need to train people quickly to improve their employment prospects. The use of technology is seen as a means of providing quick solutions to these problems. What politicians and senior education and training officials fail to realize is that technology is not a solution.

It is true that some technology trials have shown potential benefits for education and training. However, there is little evidence of long-term impact of any of these technologies. The history is that technical and electronic gadgets were 'sold' to the educational community while the technology was unproved and lacked reliability, and no consideration was given to the instructional attributes of sophisticated equipment compared to traditional teaching. Course designers and developers need to utilise technology only if it makes a contribution to education and training that is appropriate, affordable, and properly incorporated into the course design. Intelligent planning will overcome the 'flavour of the month' aspect of new technologies: for example, over the last 40 years we have seen the promotion of programmed learning, educational television, satellite delivery, computer facilitated learning, and now the CD-ROM as the panacea for all education and training ills.

These technologies do have a place in education and training. However, they need to be used alongside the traditional education and training in a cost-effective manner. The use of technology in delivery will not alone assure the quality of education and training.

The supposed 'panacea' is inviting for ministers and senior education and training officials faced with the need for 'solutions'; and 'political' decisions are influential on the source or extent of funding for courses and materials. However, the support for any course and materials delivery can change when emerging technologies attract flavour of the month of enthusiasm.

Education and training institutions have limited budgets and need to plan for the long-term when putting money into resources. Unfortunately, it is rarely the case that politicians recognize the long-term need for education and training programmes to be designed and evaluated so that the most appropriate and cost effective technology is used to support the delivery. The limited time for politicians to forward plan and implement their ideas means that they may prefer 'high profile' and therefore high technology solutions.

WHAT HAPPENS IF THERE IS A CHANGE IN COMMUNITY SUPPORT?

It is very difficult to second-guess changes in community support, particularly when the course has been developed with the support of the community of the learner.

One question that needs to be asked is whether change is a reflex reaction by some members of the community caused by influences outside of the educational community. Consider, for example, that you are about to deliver a course and materials that deal with mathematics. At about the time of delivery a national survey is released on the state of science education. As a response, the government announces new initiatives for science. What is your plan of action to see that your course and materials are not lost in the clamour for new initiative funding for science? One answer is to rewrite some publicity and talk to your educational community, indicating that your initiative can incorporate the new. Of course, if your funding is already 'in the bank', any disturbance to your programme could be minimal.

If community support changes for other reasons, you will have to consider the causes and possible recovery actions. Some of these problems are covered in the next section.

WHAT IF THE DELIVERY PROCESS GOES WRONG?

If the proper consulting process has taken place, the likelihood of problems occurring is minimized. Unfortunately, they can still happen.

The most threatening is revolt against the course and materials. This can happen at the learner level, the parent and caregiver level or even among teachers and administrators. Two courses of action are possible.

- Find someone to blame if consultation has taken place; attributing blame is more difficult. In fact, blaming someone is counterproductive to the delivery of the course and materials. It can leave everyone in a bad mood and the problem still exists.
- Find the cause.

If it seems that the delivery process is going wrong then steps should be taken to control any damage and effect a workable solution. This recovery process may well involve further consultation and revision of the course and materials.

There are other factors that can contribute to delivery problems. One is the content or context of course and materials being misconstrued, causing the 'revolt' against them. The recovery method may be to readdress the issues with the complaint, indicating the link between the course, the materials and the intended outcomes. Calm the concerns of the complainant. You may even have to consider a re-negotiation of the programme or materials. But remember that you are now negotiating with one (or a small group) of the total community. This can lead to the wider community accusing you of favouring this minority. Very soon the issue is not of teaching and learning, but of politics. The very real charge that you may face is that you are no longer impartial.

Another factor, but unfortunately a possibility, is support materials not arriving in time for the commencement of the course. What are your recovering strategies in these embarrassing circumstances? If you have the draft of the course and materials, a possible action is to begin the course using some support materials in a draft form. Or you could determine if the course materials can be derived in stages. Remember that courses are rarely initiated, studied and completed overnight. It may be sensible to stagger the delivery of the course and materials.

CONCLUSION

Document everything!

If you are faced with unexpected influences on the delivery of the new course and materials, such as a change in government or education department philosophy, or a change in the support of the educational community, you must document it all. Documentation is not just the official minutes, or correspondence; it should include the off-the-cuff comments, the 'accommodations', and any information that supports the project/course/materials, as well as those that could be a source of disagreement. With this information you are in a better position to argue for the continued support for funding and continuing support of the community.

Chapter 5
Now You Are Prepared – But What About Your Learners?

SUMMARY

You have prepared your learning materials systematically and you are ready for problems that might force you to use different delivery strategies. What should be done so the learner knows what is going on as you deliver those materials? What does the learner have to do to be able to accept the new or different methodology? What happens if that learner cannot or does not learn from this technique? How will they know, and how will the teacher know that something has gone awry? As the teacher you have to help the learner to understand the new or different delivery method so that learning can take place.

INTRODUCTION

One of the many incorrect assumptions made about learning concerns the preparation of learning materials. Often the teacher or trainer assumes that the learner is ready to accept, without question, any kind of materials and any strategy to deliver those materials. Teachers frequently express the sentiment 'The learner should understand all of this stuff and should be able to learn something... If they don't, well that's their problem'.

For the most part this might be true; there is an onus on the learner to understand and learn, and if they can't or don't, to determine how the problem can be rectified. But there is also a responsibility on the part of the teacher to help the learning to be involved in the best learning experience possible, and to do that, teachers and trainers must prepare themselves and the learners for the job they have to do in the business of learning.

This chapter is about delivery. After preparing all your learning materials, have you prepared the learner to use those materials as you deliver them?

GETTING THE MATERIALS READY

This book is concerned with the systematic delivery of learning materials. The assumption is that when you are assigned the task of materials development, you start preparing the necessary documentation that will be needed to support all the various and many decisions you will be making as the work progresses. Of course, in the real world, with its time, budget and other interested-party pressures and constraints, the best intentions for the development of learning materials often become derailed in favour of a more teacher-focused, or at least, less systematic 'let's just get it ready' approach.

However, the following discussion assumes that for the most part you have prepared your learning materials and when you did your learners were uppermost in your mind.

The delivery strategy you choose should be appropriate to the learning style of your learners.

For most people charged with the design and development of learning materials, the first thing to do is become 'more comfortable' with the topic for which are you to develop materials. Time is spent in reading and research and determining facts and formula for learner reference. As this process is taking place the beginnings of a logical progression for the delivery of the materials and the amount of material that needs to be covered also start to take shape.

As you progress, and you learn more about the materials that you are going to present, the desire to put pen to paper or fingers to computer keyboard to begin writing your materials is felt. This can take the form of lists of aims and objectives, and based on those aims and objectives, the tentative development of some initial learning materials. During this process you consciously or unconsciously consider the use of time: how much time you have, how it should be used to best advantage and how to use it in different ways.

Not long after you start developing your materials you also start thinking about some form of plan to help you determine how various parts of the learning event will unfold. The planning process gives you cause to consider and organize topics into some sort of sequence, think about the abilities and interests of your learners, and consider how you are going to deliver all the material to them.

When you are considering your delivery strategies you should consider some or all of the following:

- The traditional lecture with its introduction, new material in the middle, and a conclusion.
- The interactive lecture where the learner is asked questions or to 'shout out all you know about...'.
- Problem solving where the learner adapts current knowledge to a new learning situation.
- Demonstrations in which the learner shows proof of their skills.
- Case studies where the learner considers a real world situation or problem and provides possible solutions.
- Guided discussions in which the learner participates and expresses ideas about the topic under discussion.

As planning the delivery of materials continues, you also consider various 'real world' examples that will be inserted into the learning events to help the learner retain the most important parts. Finally you consider ways to tell the learners just what it is that you are going to do so they can plan to learn and will know if learning has taken places.

If the preceding is the process you have been following for the design and development of your learning materials, that's fine, you could do worse! There are, however, three final items that you should consider in your planning before you get to the delivery. These are, first, a methodology for the assessment of the learner. Give a lot of thought to what tests and examinations you are going to use to ascertain exactly what the learner knows; make sure they are linked very closely to your goals and objectives. Next, plan how you are going to evaluate the materials you have developed, the learning event and environment in which they will be used. Finally, go back to those plans you devised for the various parts of the event and make sure that they, at least in a small way, comply with the nine events of instruction. These events are:

A learning event should contain three elements: Telling the learner something; showing the learner something; and having the learner practise something.

1. Gaining learner attention

The most important step in any learning event is for you to focus the attention of the learner on the task at hand and try to ensure that this attention sustains their interest throughout the learning event.

2. Informing the learner of the objective

You need to inform the learner of what is going to happen during the learning event so they can focus on that event and sort out what is relevant and what is not.

3. Stimulating recall of prerequisite learning

So learners are able to put the new information into a context based on what they already know, it is important that the learning event contains something that causes them to recall a prior event, evaluate it, and use it as the foundation on which the present event will build.

4. Presenting the stimulus material

When you present the new materials it is important that you tell the learner the generalities of the operation linked to a context or background along with the facts, knowledge and skill associated with what is to be learned.

All of the above make up the *telling* portion of your learning event.

5. Providing learning guidance

One of the most important things you can do for the learner is to provide a means of encoding the information. In providing learning guidance you might show the steps involved in carrying out a task or you can suggest how the learner can complete a task.

This is the *showing* portion of your event.

6. Eliciting the performance

This is where learners are expected to respond to all that has gone on before and demonstrate their learning. It is important that this part of the event is not confused with evaluation: learners here are still learning, they are *not* being tested.

This is the *doing* portion of your event.

7. Providing feedback about performance correctness

In this part of the learning event, you give feedback to the learners so they can determine if they have performed correctly. If learning has taken place learners have to be able to judge how well they have performed according to set criteria.

8. Assessing the performance

Performance assessment is concerned with learners demonstrating their total understanding of the topic. This is the *evaluating* portion of the learning event, where you must devise a methodology to determine if the event has been successful and learning has taken place.

9. Enhancing retention and transfer

If the event has been successful the learner will be able to transfer knowledge to other situations and use it in different ways. To help ensure that this happens in an appropriate manner you must provide sufficient learning practice and feedback to the learner about their performance so any necessary adjustments can be made.

YOU ARE PREPARED – BUT IS THE LEARNER?

Your materials are prepared but the question still stands: are your learners ready? To help you answer this question, consider the following:

As you are developing your learning materials keep asking yourself the question: 'How will I know if the learners are ready to learn?'

● How do learners select, acquire and construct knowledge?
● How do learners integrate and maintain knowledge?
● How do learners retrieve knowledge?
● How do learners develop effective learning skills?

The answers depend on intellectual development of the learners; you should prepare your materials (and them) for learning according to their present stage of development. The stages of intellectual development have been described as follows:

Either/or thinking

At this stage of the learners' development there is only one right answer, knowledge is truth and the teacher is generally right. Learners will not think independently and they will not state their own point of view.

As you develop the learning materials incorporate as many real world experiences as possible into the design to help the learner categorize the learning.

Subjective knowledge

As the learner moves to this stage of development, knowledge becomes a matter of opinion. Learners begin to recognize that others like themselves have opinions and they accept all opinions as valid. Knowledge becomes contextual and situational.

Procedural knowledge

At this stage the teacher is seen as an experienced resource. Learners are beginning to be able to distinguish weak from strong evidence with respect to opinion, and knowledge is affected by values, assumptions and perspectives of the world.

Constructed knowledge

This final stage sees the learner as being able to integrate knowledge with their own experience and reflection.

Your learning events should be geared to what you perceive to be your learners' intellectual development by including activities that will help move them to higher levels of cognitive development. Try to include activities and assignments geared towards alternative perspectives and real-world experience as this will help them:

Develop their own view

For example, encourage them to

- challenge clichés
- produce evidence to support argument
- develop rational argument.

Evaluate other points of view

For example, ask your learners to

- identify criteria to help judge other points of view
- accept that not all evidence is valid.

Understand the process of judgement

For example, they should learn to

- rethink decisions
- make new decisions under different circumstances.

Determining valid information about your learners to help you make informed decisions should be done during the information gathering phase of your materials development (see *Planning a Course* in this series).

PRESENTING NEW KNOWLEDGE

When you present new knowledge you should allow that learners think, learn and process information in many different ways; learning is an individual and non-uniform process. Remember that you must inform the learner of what they are expected to learn by using such directions as 'This is important information'. Use objectives to guide the learner as to what it is they are going to do and the level of competence that they are expected to achieve. Use study questions and advanced organizers to help the learner predict what they will need to focus on as they read or interact with the materials. Provide a conceptual framework in which the learner can work.

Attending a learning event should be something the learner looks forward to. It's up to you to make it so!

Remember that previous knowledge has a great impact and influence on learning, so placing materials into a framework will help the learner pay better attention to what is being presented. Organize your materials in a way that is appropriate for learning to take place. Try to minimize distortions in the materials that will hinder the learners' progress.

As you develop your materials, ensure that they are meaningful and relevant for the learner. Consider the age of the learners, their reading ability and general outlook toward learning. Think about their interests and background and try to make viable connections between what they know and the new materials you are developing.

Limit the amount of information you give the learner and design your material so that it is delivered in manageable pieces or 'chunks'. Consider how much your learners can absorb. Avoid information overload by limiting the number of points you raise to three, four, or at the most seven. Stress concepts, not facts, as concepts are better understood and remembered.

RETAINING AND RETRIEVING NEW INFORMATION

In order for your learners to retain new information, retrieve what has already been learned, and use it in conjunction with the new information, you should provide for active learning. Learners learn best by doing. That is, by writing, discussing and otherwise taking action of some kind. Provide a way for the learners to try out what they have learned, but ensure that the environment is 'safe' – create an atmosphere where the learner feels secure and supported.

Allow the learner to apply key concepts in different situations. Provide opportunities for them to summarize, paraphrase and generalize using such strategies as role play, simulations, case studies and written assignments. Encourage cooperation and social inter-action between learners.

Consider encouraging note-taking in a classroom situation. Note-taking can increase attention and focus the learner on the materials being learned. Provide guidelines for note-taking using such tech-niques as telling them exactly what is important and what must there-fore be in their notes. You can also consider designing your materials to include skeletal notes. These notes would only list the main points you wish to cover during the learning event and encourage your learners to fill in the blank parts and make their own more detailed notes. If you give your learners notes ensure they have an obvious pattern to them so the learners themselves do not have to determine what the pattern is or even if one exists. Whatever method you choose, however, have the learners review their notes at the end of the learning event to make sure they have all the information they need.

HELPING THE LEARNER LEARN

Helping the learners learn and interact with your materials is vital to your role. Consider providing opportunities for learners to rehearse the new information they have learned through repetition. Set goals for them regarding the amount of materials they study. Stress the value of skimming and where it can and should be used. Impress on them the importance of generating questions about the materials to help them focus their studies and determine what is known and not known. Finally, give them guidelines as to when they should seek help from you and or/others.

LEARNING STYLE

As a teacher it is important that you understand the various learning styles typically adopted by the learner; this will help you make informed decisions regarding the materials you are producing. Kolb (1984) suggests grouping the many possible different styles into four typical styles, as follows.

Convergers
Convergers are learners who use abstract conceptualization and abstract experimentation as part of their thinking process. They like to find concrete answers to things and solve problems quickly.

Divergers

Divergers, on the other hand, use concrete experiences and reflective observation to generate ideas. They are often very good at brainstorming and generating alternative solutions to problems.

Assimilators

Assimilators use abstract conceptualization and observation to get a wide range of ideas, which they then make into concise logical forms. They are good at planning, development theories and creating models.

Accommodators

This final group like the concrete experience. They use active experimentation and a trial-and-error strategy to solve problems, and they tend to plunge into problems to try to arrive at an answer.

In terms of classroom activities convergers tend to prefer solving problems and having definite answers. Divergers like to involve themselves in discussion and working with others on projects. Assimilators like to participate in the action through role play and simulation. And accommodators like hands-on activities. To successfully design and develop learning materials, you as a teacher need to observe and understand the different needs of different learners.

Evaluating learning

To help both you and the learner work together in a conducive learning environment you may wish to consider developing an evaluation instrument whereby learners can observe their own learning style and preferences. This will help them to better understand their role in relation to the materials you are presenting to them, but it will also help them to recognize what role they will have to play in dealing with other learning materials. They will be able to ascertain the most productive learning strategy for themselves and where they will feel most comfortable.

As a teacher or trainer you also need to recognize your own style and how it influences the materials you develop and the way you deliver them. Do not try to match your style with that of learners, rather try to work with the learners in a way that is best for everybody. Be sensitive to issues such as ethnicity, gender, parents and other background influences, as well as learning style, as all are likely to impact on the learner.

There is a number of good learning style inventories on the market that make it fun for the learner to complete. Don't be afraid to try some out.

Try to use a variety of teaching aids when delivering your learning materials. This way learners will not become bored.

Learning strategies and delivery methodologies

As was noted at the start of this chapter, you need to vary, as much as possible, your delivery methodologies. The more often you present the stimulus material to the learner using different tools, and the more often you provide some learning guidance to elicit performance, the more likely you will enhance retention and the transfer of learning to new real-world situations.

CONCLUSION

This chapter has discussed some of the issues associated with both getting you ready to deliver learning materials and the learner ready to work with those materials and learn from them.

A lot of thought should be given to the intellectual development of the learner and how they get, retain and use new information. There are four basic learning styles, and as a teacher you should learn and understand as much as you can about learning styles to help you better design and develop viable learning materials. Try as much as possible to vary your delivery strategy, call on the learner to think in different ways and encourage them to value different styles of learning and teaching. You should help learners to develop different thinking processes and appreciate other delivery methods as a way to prepare themselves for learning.

Chapter 6
Instructional Events

SUMMARY

The common denominators of teaching are telling, showing and doing. How you might use each method is explained in this chapter and examples are given as to where each can be used. 'Putting it all together' discusses how to use most effectively the tell, show and do methods during a learning event.

INTRODUCTION

When you are about to teach a topic to a group of learners how do you pass on the information? What are the choices you have to deliver the content? Whether you are teaching using mass, group or individualized instruction, you have only three choices. The learners can be told the information, be shown how to use it or allowed to use the information to undertake an activity. These are the common denominators of teaching and organizing course content.

Telling, showing and doing

As an example, if you are teaching biology, an objective might be: 'At the completion of the lesson the learners should be able to identify the main components of the mammalian heart'. How can you teach this? You only have three choices:

- telling
- showing
- doing.

Telling

The learners can be *told* the information, ie given the names of each component part, told what it does and where it is located.

Showing

The learners could be shown diagrams and models of the heart showing the location of each part. Or the teacher could perform a dissection on a mammal heart and show the learners the location of each part.

Doing

The teacher could allow the learners to dissect a mammal's heart for themselves, and have them identify each of the parts.

What is the best method to teach your subject? Think back to when you were a learner and ask yourself which was the most effective way you learned. Did you learn best when you were told something, shown something or were able to practise the skill? You will probably come to the conclusion that you learned most effectively when the teacher applied all three techniques.

Take another example. When teaching scuba diving the learning objective might be: 'The learner should be able to correctly attach a scuba regulator to an air tank'. How would you teach this in terms of the common denominators? Two methods are appropriate.

Method 1

Telling and showing. Show and tell the learners how to attach the regulator to the tank. Often the tell and show methods are combined.

Doing. Allow the learners to practise the skill. They would attach a scuba regulator to an air tank while the teacher supervised.

Method 2

Telling and showing. Explain and show how to attach the regulator to the tank in a series of steps.

1. Unscrew the dust cap.
2. Check the filter.
3. Place the yoke over the tank outlet.
4. Check there is an O-ring in the tank outlet.
5. Place the yoke against the outlet and tighten the screw.
6. Turn on the air.

7. Turn the pressure gauge away from you.
8. Check that air comes out of the mouth piece when the purge button
   is depressed.

Doing. The learners would complete each task as it is shown by the
teacher. To ensure the learners can attach the regulator by themselves,
they would be asked to repeat the exercise.

Whether you use the first or the second depends on the complexity
of the task you are teaching. With simple tasks you would use
method 1: tell and show at the same time, followed by the do component. For more complex tasks you can break down the tell and show
methods into a series of small steps, followed by the do component.

THE TELL METHODS

Whether you are using mass, group or individualized instruction, you
can apply the basic techniques of telling. Telling is often considered a
form of mass instruction, such as a lecture, but this need not be the
case. Telling the learners can mean passing the knowledge using print
material or computer-based training or any other type of medium. It is
not necessarily done orally.

Examples of telling

Telling methods include:

Make sure that
the materials
you are 'telling'
to the learners
is broken into
small
manageable
chunks.

- lectures
- group-based types of instruction such as discussions
- self-instructional texts
- textbooks
- radio and television broadcasts and videotapes
- computer-based training.

Telling methods often include the use of teaching aids, if the telling
is done by the teacher, and may involve computers or other audio-
visual technology. The type of telling method you use depends on
the type of delivery you are using. This has been outlined in *Planning
a Course*.

For example, if you are going to explain to your students the
principles of Boyle's gas law you could do so in the following ways.

Method 1

'Boyle's law states that the pressure of a gas is inversely proportional to its volume at constant temperature. Therefore, when the surrounding pressure of a gas in a flexible container is decreased the volume will expand, provided the temperature is kept constant.'

Method 2

'When you go scuba diving you must remember the principle of Boyle's gas law, if you don't you could die. When you are breathing compressed air at a depth and begin to ascend you must continue to breathe normally. If you hold your breath the compressed air in your lungs will expand due to the reduced surrounding pressure and there is a danger that your lungs could rupture.

'This can be explained by Boyle's gaw law, which states that at constant temperature, the pressure of a gas is inversely proportional to the volume of the gas. Therefore, if you reduce the pressure surrounding your lungs by ascending, the volume of the air will expand. If you don't exhale your lungs could rupture. Many scuba divers have died because they did not remember or comprehend Boyle's gas law.'

Both these examples tell the same facts, but the second tells it in a more interesting way. Just because you are using a telling method does not mean that it cannot be interesting.

When you use the telling method, don't assume that because you have told the learners the facts once that they understand it. Follow the old rule that public speakers use:

Telling learners once is not enough! Remember the old saying – tell people what you are about to say – Say it, then tell people what you have just said.

● tell them what you are going to tell them
● then tell them
● then summarize what you have told them.

Using the tell methods

Here are some ways of making telling more effective.

● Tell the facts in a story form.
● Use your own experiences to make the facts interesting.
● Elaborate on the facts you are telling them.
● Summarize in point form.
● Question the learners on what you have told them.
● Make the students do exercises using what you have told them.

These guidelines can be used whether you are telling them directly or via other media.

THE SHOW METHODS

Showing methods allows the learners to see the steps required to achieve the objectives of the lesson.

Examples might be to show the learners how to: make a dove-tail joint; use a microscope; use a circular saw; perm hair; or make a flower arrangement.

It is easy to *tell* learners how to do these things, but it is more effective to *show* and *tell* them. Unfortunately, teachers may avoid the show methods because they take too much time, but in the long run it allows for more effective learning.

For example, a floristry teacher has problems showing learners how to make a wedding bouquet as it would take at least one hour for the demonstration, one and a half hours for the learners to make the bouquet, but the class itself is only two hours long.

The solution to the problem is to use teaching aids. A video of the demonstration could be made and edited to ten minutes duration, showing learners the entire process. A flip card booklet could be produced to show the process in a series of step-by-step, colour photographs. Learners could then follow the steps given in the flip cards as they produced their own bouquet.

Tell and show method

The show method depends on showing images, so there are a variety of ways of doing it. Usually the tell and show methods are used in conjunction with each other. For example, the teacher can show an overhead transparency of a transducer and explain the function of each part. Little would be gained by the learners if they just saw the overhead transparency of the transducer.

Examples of showing

Below are listed some of the methods and equipment you can use to show materials.

- blackboard
- photographs
- computer presentations
- slides
- models
- felt boards
- videos
- role playing
- overhead projectors
- posters
- real items
- experiments
- simulations
- demonstrations.

Show methods can involve concrete objects or abstract concepts. You can use real objectives to show things. For example, you could use an actual fuel injector to show its parts rather than using a diagram. You can use a wide variety of show methods to teach abstract concepts. For example, a computer simulation model could be used to demonstrate the Law of Diminishing Returns. The objectives you are trying to teach will assist you to select the appropriate show method.

Using the show method

Make sure that your show method does not confuse the learners by keeping it simple and breaking it down into small manageable 'chunks'.

If you are going to use showing, it is vital that whatever you show is clear and does not confuse learners. Follow these guidelines.

- Ensure that the visual is visible, whether you are making a presentation to a class or to an individual.
- Ensure that the visual is the right size for your function. For example, ensure the text on your transparency can be read by everyone in the class.
- Check that all the equipment that you are using is operational.
- Move at the appropriate speed for your learners, whether giving a demonstration or running a video.

THE DO METHODS

To consolidate learning use a 'do' method.

Telling and showing the learners information does not mean that the learners have learned the subject matter. The learners must be given an opportunity to apply or use this information.

For example, if you are shown and told how to do cardiopulmonary resuscitation, can you actually do it? To ensure that you can, it must be practised. Just being told and shown is not enough.

Many teachers are confused about what the do method involves. They might say their learners are *doing* when they are answering questions in class and answering written questions or completing a test. This might be true in some cases, but not in all.

If you are teaching mathematics, the learners must complete problems related to the topic being taught. If they are being taught writing they must practise their writing and not just answer questions about writing. It is a little easier to see the relationship between what the learners should do with practical skills. For example, if the learners are told and shown how to weld a flange, then they must practise welding a flange to ensure that they have learned the skill.

People are active learners. Even if the teacher tells and shows learners in an interesting way, they will become bored if they are not involved in the learning. The do methods are essential to reinforce learning where the learners apply what they have been shown and told. The do method must be applied to all learners, not just a few. Asking questions in the class does not involve all learners unless they all answer questions. The do method must be applied to all courses and must be part of each learning experience.

Make sure that your do methods involve *all* the people in the group.

Examples of doing

There is a wide variety of do methods; a few examples are listed below. Some of these could also be used for show and tell methods.

People are active learners, so make your materials active and give your learners something to do.

- seminars
- brainstorming
- field trips
- simulations
- group activities
- case studies
- workshops
- debates

- experiments
- role plays
- seminars
- games
- projects
- discussion groups
- surveys
- practical work

The type of do method you use will depend on the instructional objectives of your teaching. Do methods do not have to be complicated; they can be as simple as note taking and small group discussions. The amount of activity will depend on the content you are delivering.

When learners are doing something in the classroom they are actively involved in the lesson content. It gives the teachers an opportunity to see how well they have understood what they have been shown and told. If the learners are doing in the classroom they will be able to see what they don't understand and can ask the teacher relevant questions.

PUTTING IT ALL TOGETHER

When you are delivering your lesson you must always include tell, show and do methods. You can do this in many different formats.

Telling and showing, then doing

For example, if you want to teach your students how to make a flower arrangement you could use the following sequence.

Tell   Explain how to make a flower arrangement.
Show   Show a video on how to make a flower arrangement.
Do   Let the learners practise making a flower arrangement.

You could break your objective into sub-objectives if the subject matter you are teaching is complex as in the example below.

Telling, showing, doing

If you wanted your learners to bisect a right angle using a protractor, you could plan to teach it as follows:

Skill steps	Tell	Show	Do
1. Place the protractor on the horizontal line.	Tell and show how to place the protractor on the horizontal line.		Have the students place the protractor on the line.
2. Find the 45 degrees on the protractor.	Explain why 45 degrees is chosen.	Show the 45 degree point.	Have the students locate the 45 degree point.
3. Mark the 45 degree points.	Explain why it is important to mark the point.	Show them how to mark the point.	Have the students mark the point.
4. Draw a line between the mark and where the lines intersect.	Tell and show how to draw the line.		Have the students draw the line.

Figure 6.1   *A tell-show-do teaching plan*

A variation on the above would be for the teachers to tell and show the entire task and then have the learners practise it.

CONCLUSION

In this chapter the delivery has been broken down into three basic elements: telling, showing and doing. All teaching and learning should be broken down this way, no matter how complex the subject matter being taught. Each element is important but, as we have seen, using all three elements is the most effective way to assist learners to learn. Too often teachers only tell and show learners the content. They do not use the do method. Teachers may think they are using a do method by setting an assignment, but it may not be related directly to what is being taught. The do methods are an essential part of keeping the learners involved and assisting them to learn.

Chapter 7
Interaction with a Purpose

SUMMARY

In Chapter 1 methods of opening up a closed setting were described. This chapter concentrates on how interactions can be developed in an open setting and be included in your instructional materials. It shows you how to deliver learning materials incorporating quality interactions, explains why interactions are important, defines quality interactions and describes the different types of interactions that can occur. This chapter also explains how interactions are used and how they can be improved.

INTRODUCTION

When two people interact they usually talk, but interaction can also take place in many other ways, such as through facial expression and body language. In a more traditional teaching setting when a teacher and learners interact they usually talk to each other. Perhaps the teacher asks a question and a learner answers. When this occurs interaction has taken place.

Interactions usually involve at least two participants. In a learning setting these could be a teacher and learner or a learner and peer. A learner may have interactions that relate to their studies with their family and friends. There are also times when learners interact with themselves. For example, if the learner is using self-directed material or open learning material this may contain questions in the text to provoke an internal debate.

Interaction is very important in learning. Be sure to include some form of interaction in the delivery of your learning materials.

A question to promote internal debate

If you were to be asked, as you read this, a question such as: 'Do you think it is possible for a learner to argue with themself the merits of embedded questions in text?' how would you respond? You might want to consider if there are merits such as reinforcing new information, or demerits such as interrupting the flow of concentration on the course content.

LEARNING AND INTERACTION

Learning is an active process. In order to learn a person has to take part in various learning activities. Interaction is an essential element of learning. For example, interactions have to take place even in distance learning. Here the learners often study in isolation; they have a limited chance to interact directly with teachers and tutors. However, they interact through assignments, tele-conferencing and study schools. Not all interactions have to be with another person. If learners can not interact with the learning materials they will not learn. Interaction with learning materials can be promoted by identifying the learning materials that learners find most involving and encouraging interaction between them and those materials.

> Try to provide your learners with as wide a variety of interactions as possible.

The network of interactions

The various people the learners interact with can be divided into different categories. The traditional interaction network between the learners and others is shown in Figure 7.1. This illustrates a traditional educational environment where the teacher is the main source of information. An indication of the frequency of contact between the components and the learner is indicated by the thickness of the lines. There are many other interactions involved, but the major ones are shown. The model would probably be better represented by a three dimension matrix as interactions involved in learning are very complex. For example, the learner could interact with the teacher who is also a friend, and the learning provider may be the learner's employer or the institution where learning takes place. Thus some of the components will be more important to different learners' studies than others.

Figure 7.2 shows a network of interactions for an independent learner. In this situation learners will interact more with instructional

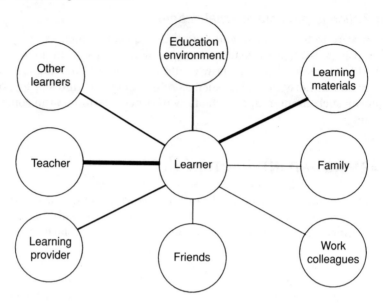

Figure 7.1   *The traditional learner's network of interactions*

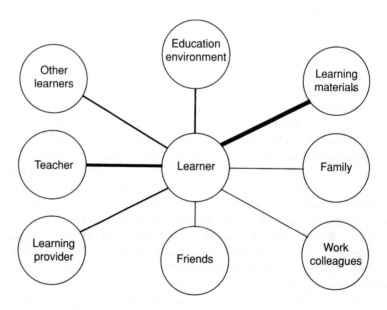

Figure 7.2   *The independent learner's network of interactions*

materials and less with the teacher. Learners study from independent learning materials that have interactions built into them for effective learning to occur. Ways to develop interactions with the traditional methods of instruction are discussed in *Planning a Course* and *Preparing a Course*.

Many educational and training organizations around the world have moved or are moving to a competency based system of education and training. This shift also places the learners and their needs in the centre of the education and training community.

The most important interactions

If learners are studying in an open setting the main components they interact with are the learning materials and the teacher. In some cases they interact with work colleagues. For example, if the learner is a teacher studying for a higher degree in education his or her interactions with colleagues will become very important to development.

Quality interactions in learning materials

When delivering courses it is important for you to build in quality interactions for your learners. The quality of the educational experience is just as important as what the learners learn.

When you design an interaction make sure it is useful to the learner and is not a time waster.

Quality can be described as the appropriateness of the programme to the required purpose and to a certain standard. What are the elements of quality in an open learning setting? These will vary depending on the type of course, learners and many other factors. Here are a few examples:

- the flexibility to organize study around life commitments
- a well organized and structured study programme
- properly constructed learning materials
- the opportunity to interact with staff and peers
- teachers who make themselves available to learners
- a study workload that is manageable
- a consistent and balanced formal assessment.

LEARNING MEDIA

Try to provide a variety of media for your learners as this will add interest to the learning event.

There are many different types of resource with which learners interact. These include print, audio-tape, computers and videos. All have different advantages and disadvantages, but the predominant medium used in study is still print. It follows, therefore, that if you can improve the interactivity of your text-based learning materials, you can improve the chances of the learners learning in both open and closed learning settings. Interactions should be built into print-based materials when you are planning and writing.

In-text questions

Text can be made more interactive through in-text questions. These are not assessable, but allow the learners to interact with the text. They are included at regular interviews in the text and usually the answers are not given. Thus if learners don't know the answer they are expected to re-read the relevant section of the text. However, for technical subjects answers should be given, especially when exact or numerical answers are required. Some subjects need more practice and hence more in-text questions; these include mathematics, physics, chemistry, language, accountancy and computer science.

Here are some points to bear in mind when writing effective in-text questions:

Make sure that your in-text questions are appropriate and in the right place in the materials.

- Motivate the reader by asking interesting questions.
- Make questions helpful by clarifying and expanding important points in the text.
- Offer a challenge, ie, ask the learner to undertake a task.
- Write the questions at the correct level of difficulty. Being able to answer correctly builds up the student's confidence – too complicated a question could destroy confidence.
- Questions should be directly applicable to the content of the unit and facilitate the understanding of it.
- Questions should be written in an informal, user-friendly tone.

Other points about in-text questions, along with examples, are:

- Questions should enable learners to assess their own progress and understanding. You might write text similar to 'At the beginning of this section it was stated that you would be introduced to the concepts of fields in a database. Did you understand these concepts before? How confident are you to use the concepts in discussion with others now?'
- Questions should be linked to an objective. If an objective of the course is that the learner will be able to specify the requirements of

a database, a question could be 'Provide a brief rationale specifying the fields in a data-base for client contact'.

● Use two simple questions rather than one complex question. Complex questions can confuse rather than clarify issues. For example, the following is too complex: 'What types of information would you need to prepare the specification of a database recording client information?' The following is better: 'List the information you would require to develop a database of clients. From that list identify the key identifiers that you would need to generate reports'.

Care should be used in designing in-text questions and the number you place in the text. If there are too many, or if they are too difficult to answer, the learners may not complete them. However, well designed in-text questions will improve the interactivity of text.

Remember that a well-designed in-text question is difficult for the learner to ignore.

Making text accessible

Learners will have more interactions with the learning materials if they are organized so that the information is presented clearly and is readable. Here are a few ways of presenting your information clearly and encouraging more learning interactions.

Objectives

Objectives should be given at the outset. They inform the learners about what they should be able to do when the instruction is over. They are also useful as advance organizers.

Advance organizers

These indicate the ways in which new material will be the same as, or different from, what the students already know. They are helpful in clarifying conceptual issues. A glossary of key words can be used effectively as advance organizers. There are several types of advance organizers. For example, a table of contents indicates to the learner how the material is organized in advance of their reading it. However advance organizers may also serve as links.

Titles of units

The titles of units should contain as few words as possible to describe the content of the text.

Headings

Headings in the text orient the learners. A sub-heading structure is essential to map the course of learning. Headings written in the form of a statement or question can help interactivity.

Summaries

Summaries help the student recall and understand the body of the text by listing the main points or drawing them together in concluding comments.

In-text questions

In-text questions given at the beginning of a passage, or given before paragraphs of relevant material, help the learner to read with a specific learning objective.

Sequencing

Position illustrations, graphs, tables next to or close to where they are mentioned in the text. Readers can lose their thread if they have to search for illustrative material.

Text design

Text is more readable if it is broken into smaller paragraphs, aligned left (not-justified), and the typeface is clear and an appropriate size. Key words and concepts can be highlighted – but don't distract the reader with too much **bold** and *italic*.

INTERACTION WITH THE TEACHER

The minimum involvement of a teacher in an open setting is to mark the learners' work and suggest what is wrong with it. Often this is done by written comments. There are many ways of making these comments more effective for the learner.

- Comments should motivate the learners by encouraging them to engage in thinking, reading and other activities related to the topic under study.
- Create a friendly atmosphere between yourself and the learners. Don't adopt a threatening or over-formal tone.
- Start your comments from where the learners are now rather than offering model answers.

- Respect learners' feelings and give their answers consideration, especially when they do not agree with your own.
- Be specific with criticism.
- Make your comments legible – unreadable notes are of no use to learners.
- Suggest alternative approaches or interpretations that learners could use.
- Use positive feedback: point out improvement by comparing the student's present and previous work.
- Use a colour other than red for marking. Many learners have had bad learning experiences from this colour and react adversely to it!
- Comment on any special insight the learners have given.
- Mention the good points as well as the poor points in learners' work.
- Mark and return work as quickly as possible.
- Encourage learners to contact you to discuss your comments.

CONCLUSION

The learning experience of the learner can be improved through quality interaction. This can be done by developing the interactivity of the text-based learning materials, and encouraging better interaction between the teacher and learner.

Chapter 8
Letting Go: The Transfer of Knowledge

SUMMARY

Teachers are subject matter experts. When they teach their particular discipline it may seem that students do not appreciate the knowledge they are gaining. However, there comes a point when they have to sanction the expertise gained by the learner. What happens when the teacher is not confident of the ability of a learner, even when the learner has 'passed'? When the ability of the learner is formally recognized, he or she has the right to exercise ownership of the knowledge and skills gained as a newly sanctioned expert. This chapter examines some of the issues of ownership of knowledge and the increasing uses of technology to pass on knowledge.

INTRODUCTION

The ownership of course content and the transfer of ownership to the learner need to be reviewed at the time of delivery. This chapter addresses the following points.

- The transfer of knowledge from teacher to learner.
- The teaching alternatives offered by technology.
- Recognizing life experience and prior learning.
- The threat to teachers.

TRANSFER OF KNOWLEDGE: TEACHER TO LEARNER

Teachers may feel threatened by the learner being able to 'act' as competently as themselves. If that seems a strange concept, consider the role of the parent as a responsible caregiver and participant in the education of a learner, and the role of the teacher in relation to the same learner.

For the parents or caregivers, rites of passage of the child are a challenge as each represents a milestone in the development of the child. For a teacher, the demonstration of appropriate skills and knowledge by the learner could give rise to a rite of passage that confronts the teacher. In this situation teachers should recognize the learner's development and trust their learners as achieving and being as informed as themselves.

An example is the teachering of $1 + 1 = 2$, which seems straightforward. The complications arise when you attempt to add 'unlike' entities. On one level a learner may match their teacher in that they can add similar entities. However, on a more complex level the learner may be different to their teacher in that they are unable to comprehend that:

1 apple + 1 orange =

either 1 apple or 1 orange

or 2 pieces of fruit

There are subtle differences in the answers. Two unlike items cannot be added: an apple is not an orange, therefore they cannot be added together to form one thing. But, two unlike things can be made alike by being given a broader classification. Therefore, if we look more generically at 'apple' and 'orange' it is possible to arrive at the classification of 'fruit', and the addition of fruit is possible. The ability of the learner to arrive at both answers, or two 'correct' answers, is significant in terms of the cognitive process. The sophistication shown by arriving at two answers is similar to that of the teacher. Will the teacher accept either or both answers? If so, how does the teacher interpret the answers? While the answers demonstrate the cognitive ability of the learner, there follows the teacher's ability to understand and evaluate the learner's cognitive functions. Unless there is some other test information, by which the teacher can determine how the learner arrived at the answers, the teacher cannot confidently assess the learner's cognitive skills.

LEARNING POSSIBILITIES OFFERED BY TECHNOLOGY

Technology has played a role in education and training. However, it is becoming increasingly possible to access information through non-traditional sources. If schools and libraries are considered traditional sources of information, then Internet bulletin boards are currently non-traditional. But the possibilities offered by electronic access to information are considerable and not without the potential for information overload.

It should be noted that electronic access to information does raise issues.

- There are socio-economic limits to the availability of resources such as computers.
- There could be problems with the ability of learners to use the information that is available to them through electronic means.
- The availability of technology in the work place or the home is a possible factor in the individual taking a more proactive role in their personal development. As such, it is possible that the availability of electronic means of education and training will be a means of developing independent learners.
- Does access to information for an independent learner change the 'power' relationship between the learner and teacher?
- What happens about recognition of the learner's learning through these electronic means? In other words how does the learner gain credit for their learning? This could lead to institutions needing to set up mechanisms, which may be costly, to verify the learner's learning.

All these factors will need to be considered if the use of technology and electronic information systems are to be part of the delivery options.

RECOGNITION OF LIFE EXPERIENCE AND PRIOR LEARNING

Until recently people without formal education or formal training could be said to lack skills. The assumptions about how knowledge and skills are gained are now changing. The distinction between formal skills gained through education and training and abilities gained through the experiences of living, as a skill-building process, is becoming credible. One of the biggest causes of the change are those in charge of formal education. It is becoming increasingly accepted that people without formal education and training are able to demonstrate skills that are equivalent to skills gained through completion of part of a formal education and training course.

The processes involved in recognition – prior learning, credit transfers, advanced standing because of demonstrated competence and variations on these – are still evolving and seem complex. But over time recognition of learning and life skills will become an accepted part of education and training. This is happening already.

At the delivery stage, institutions and teachers will have to deal with requests for prior learning to be assessed. This will happen increasingly as recognition becomes more widely known as an option for gaining credits or exemption and possibly shortening the learner's time in a course.

Think about some of the situations where recognition might arise.

- Do teachers in early education recognize the prior learning of a child, when from birth to enrolment in the pre-school, the activities undertaken by the child lacked formal structure? How do teachers assess this prior learning?
- When learners move between stages of formal education, how much of their prior learning goes unrecognized? In other words, how much re-teaching is undertaken when there may be no need, or is this revision?
- Why is that the content of many first-year university courses replicates work supposedly done in the final years of school, or is this just revision too?

There is perhaps a need to ask not what the learner has experienced but what the learner is capable of doing because of the experience. This is recognition of the learner's skills, knowledge and abilities, of the experiences they can use in practice.

For the individual learner, there may be practical reasons why they want their skills acknowledged, apart from the frustration of repeating learning. For example, a person may have current skills but want their skills recognized so they will gain more pay. How does this cut across your course or materials and the delivery? Have you planned for delivery options?

The skills, abilities and knowledge a person has are an amalgam of formal education, training and life experiences. These life experiences may relate to interpersonal matters and possibly affect the attitude towards learning and the ability to learn. The case study that follows represents one example of life experience outweighing formal training.

Case study

The manager of a small company needed a secretary and advertised in the local papers. The manager shortlisted four applicants. As a result of the interviews it was decided that two applicants were in close contention.

The dilemma about selecting between the top two candidates was resolved by referring to typing speeds. The manager reluctantly telephoned the candidate with the slower typing speed, to inform this person that they had not been successful. But the manager was greeted with a very pleasant, welcoming voice. Only then did the manager realize that what the company needed more than a secretary with a high typing speed was someone to answer the telephone in a friendly and helpful manner. Hasty consultation was needed, but the company ended up with a very presentable image over the phone. And the letters requiring high-speed typing skills? These are produced as required, with accuracy and on time.

This story is true. It is used here to indicate that even when a person (a learner) has passed a course it may be other skills, beyond those 'imparted' by the course, that lead to the learner's success after education and training. It may be that at the time of delivery attention should also focus on the attributes of the learner and on encouraging a foundation for developing these beyond the course. This recognizes that some learning may be job related but learning is an ongoing process.

OH... AND THE THREAT!

Early in this chapter the issue of a threat to teachers by developing the expertise of learners was raised. Some teachers may feel that their 'standing' as a subject expert is threatened by a learner who is becoming an expert in their subject.

But possibly the threat is just the opposite. The danger to teachers is that they guard their expertise too closely. If education and training take place in a 'community of learning', it can only benefit the teacher to be open and generous with their knowledge. If teachers remain too closed, learners may seek other means of learning, such as through technology or moving to a different (possibly more responsive) education and training organization. By protecting their knowledge teachers may threaten their own role.

CONCLUSION

This chapter has looked at some of the aspects of course delivery, with a focus on the relationship between the teacher as a subject expert and the learners developing a similar expertise. In part that has to do with several aspects of recognition. First is the recognition by the teacher that the learner is gaining expertise through the formal course. Then there are the possibilities of the learner gaining expertise through the independent use of technology; while there are issues in the use of technology. At the same time it is possible that issues of recognizing prior learning and experience may affect the delivery of a course and materials. In some cases the development of the expertise of the learner may be seen as a threat to the 'standing' of the teacher – but a teacher who jealously guards their own expertise may threaten their own role.

Chapter 9
Computer Managed Learning

SUMMARY

This chapter is an overview of computer managed learning and how it is used as a management tool in an open learning or individualized learning environment. Computer managed learning or CML is a course management tool defined as the use of the computer to solve instructional management problems.

INTRODUCTION

Computer managed learning is a management tool, not a computer based learning system that delivers course materials to the learner. Having said that, with the advent of the World Wide Web some CML applications are now designed to deliver course materials. Primarily, however, computer managed learning programmes are designed to assist large groups of learners, teachers and administration staff cope with the inherent problems of tracking learners through a series of individualized learning events.

When you are considering a CML software package make sure that it manages the learner and does not just present test items.

A CML system is a management tool that helps you identify a path for your learners to follow through a series of learning events and, based on that path, tracks their progress and tests their achievement.

Both you and your learners would typically access a CML program from stand alone computers, local area networks and the World Wide Web.

When learners complete your computer or paper based assignment they are presented with a series of test items. The learner answers the questions either on- or off-line and the computer marks it. This way learners can receive immediate feedback from you and in some cases you can provide individual comments on each of their answers.

Computer managed learning has many benefits for you and the learner as well as for those in charge of your institution or organization.

For your learners the typical benefits include:

- a graphic interface where he or she can access your assessments
- better access to you and the various learning resources you have provided
- 'quality' contact time with you
- immediate feedback from you on tests and assignments, thus creating a more confident learner
- the opportunity to work from home, organization or office
- access to the World Wide Web
- a non judgmental system with respect to his or her responses
- access by both on- and off-campus learners.

For you the benefits include:

- a greater opportunity for you to personalize the learning experience
- the recognition of prior learning, such that you can program the system to deliver only the relevant materials and assessment
- the adaptation of the system to your learner's learning speed, learning style and knowledge level
- the opportunity for you to engage in a more productive interaction with learners in the actual learning environment
- the ability to use the curriculum design component of the system to ensure the learners are always directed towards the current objective
- the ability to have sound, video and animation files as part of your tests and assignments
- the ability to launch other computer programs
- the provision of a valid and reliable resting procedure
- use of an automatic, detailed record keeping system
- appropriate access both to enrichment and remedial materials
- the early identification of learner difficulties
- the issuing and marking of objective tests.

For administration the benefits include:

- the standardization of a delivery methodology and testing procedure
- the reduction of learner failure through the early identification of learner problems
- consistent monitoring of the learner's progress
- more efficient monitoring of both distance and on campus learners
- increased efficiency
- the delivery of instruction and assessment over a local area network and the World Wide Web.

CML offers both you and the institution a viable methodology for tracking learners through a series of diverse 'individual' learning activities each taking place at different times and locations both inside and outside the organization. Using this type of delivery methodology and supporting the various activities with other appropriate interaction when required, you are now free to act as a facilitator of the teaching, learning process.

CML is a very efficient management tool for courses delivered over the World Wide Web. The World Wide Web can be set up to deliver instructional materials to the learners and CML set up to allow learners to 'practise' what they have learned and receive immediate feedback.

A CML COURSE

A CML course usually consists of a test bank that contains various test items and a course map (testing strategy) that details the assignments or tests you are going to give the learner. Some of the newer CML systems also have an instructional component, but this is more common to those systems designed specifically to be used in conjunction with the World Wide Web.

Remember that many subjective tests can be rewritten as objective items without too much trouble.

Types of items used in CML

You can use any type of test item in a CML system, however, the most suitable are objective type items that can be marked by the computer.

You can also include subjective type items in your item bank but you will have to mark them off-line and enter the mark into the learner's record. The most suitable CML test items are:

- multiple-choice
- true/false
- short (one or two word) answer
- mathematical random number generation.

Your test items can include text, equations, special symbols and graphics as well as sound, animation and in some cases video. Many CML programs also allow the learner to launch other applications such as word processing and CD-ROM training programs. This gives you the added advantage of adding these resources to your test items.

Most CML programs allow you to give some form of remedial comment for each question. This way the learners will not only know if they have the correct answer, but they can also receive a reinforcing comment. Conversely, if they choose an incorrect option you can provide some form of 'corrective' feedback.

It is of critical importance that your test items be well written to ensure validity at all levels. Many of the better CML programs are able to provide item analysis in the program itself to help you determine the validity and reliability of the test items. Other systems, however, only provide you with various data which then have to be uploaded into a commercial statistics application for analysis. The writing of test items used in the CML environment is no different from writing test items for the classroom. The chapter on writing test items in Book 4 of this series should give you more assistance in this area.

Course map

As you develop your test bank you must also determine your testing strategy and set up that strategy using the course map facility provided by the program.

Most CML programs provide you with a great deal of control regarding how you can present assignments to your learners. You should note here that in many CML systems both tests and examinations are referred to as assignments because of the adverse reaction some learners have to the words 'tests' and 'examinations'.

Some of the decisions you will have to make when designing your CML assessment strategy are:

- How often will the learners need to complete a CML assignment?
- How much material should I cover in each CML assignment?

When you are designing your testing strategies sit down with the subject matter experts and ask them what it is that they want regarding a test strategy. Their views are important!

- How many different types of assignment should I use? For example, non assessable, in-course assessments and end-of-course assessment.
- How should I design each CML assignment? For example, what pass mark should I assign, how many times can learners attempt the assignment, how many questions should I include and which objectives should I assess?

A typical CML program may have some or all of the following features. These features help you implement the assessment strategy properly:

- the ability for you to determine the level of learner mastery
- the amount of time your learners have to complete the assignment
- whether your learners need to be supervised during the assignment
- whether you need to release this particular assignment to your learners or allow them to download it themselves
- the ability for you to include other instructional materials in the assignment
- the maximum number of attempts you want your learners to have before they pass the assignment
- the ability for you to decide when or if to give your learners an automatic pass
- the ability for you to assign questions at different levels of difficulty
- the ability for you to decide on the number of questions in the assignment
- giving the learner the choice of completing the assignment on- or off-line.

LEARNER INTERACTION WITH CML

Learners can have many kinds of interactions with a CML system. At its most basic level it can guide your learners sequentially through a set of predefined activities that make up their module or unit of study. Using this method the learner first completes any learning activities. These activities can include reading a textbook, viewing a video, performing an experiment, using the World Wide Web to search for information and/or viewing a computer based training program. These activities are developed using a standard stimulus/response (SR) approach to learning so your learners receive feedback regarding the concept being studied to ensure it has been mastered before they go on to the next activity.

Following the learning activity or activities the next step might be for your learners to log on to the CML system and request a computer generated assignment based on the study guide materials. The system then generates the request and the learner completes the assignment as determined by the course map.

If it is an unsupervised assignment it will be automatically released to your learners. If it is an assignment that requires your supervision you will have to release it before it can be completed by the learner.

Once your learners complete the assignment the computer then marks each item and records the score, the items used from the item pool, the items answered correctly, and those answered incorrectly. The computer then displays an assignment report. This report indicates the percentage your learner achieved on the test, the items that were answered incorrectly and the learner's answers, and the correct answers. If learners achieve the predefined standard you have set they are allowed to proceed to the next assignment. If the standard is not achieved they will be expected to review the course materials and redo the assignment before proceeding. When learners feel ready for the next assignment they can request one from the system. This cycle is repeated until the module or unit is completed.

YOUR INTERACTION WITH A TYPICAL CML SYSTEM

Your interaction with a CML system can be classified as one of three functions; clerical, report generation and system management. The clerical function includes such things as you registering learners on the system, allowing them access to other parts of the system, finding passwords, changing marks and performing other basic tasks.

Report generation has you performing tasks such as checking report card grades, learner histories and reviewing the analysis of both your questions and learning objectives. The system can also be used to identify learners according to specific criteria such as those experiencing difficulty mastering a specific objective. This allows you to identify learners for diagnostic purposes. System management functions include things such as making changes to predefined course sequences and other course decisions. However, at this level, as a 'teacher' your access to the system might be restricted by your organization's computer department to ensure the testing strategy and course map remains consistent for all learners.

CML AND OPEN LEARNING

The modular aspect of open learning packages implies that they are stand-alone units that can be studied on or off campus at a pace appropriate to the learner's needs. Make sure that you design them in that way.

Open learning helps provide your learners with new dimensions for learning in that they are able to access a wider range of learning materials because of the ability to track what they are doing and what they have completed.

Computer managed learning is also very helpful in the administration of open learning programmes and provides the management tools needed to support such an undertaking.

Record keeping and record generation is one of the most important functions in the management of open learning, in fact it has been suggested that the primary reason for the emergence of CML was a recognition of the unmanageability of highly unitized, rate of progress, individualized instructional schemes.

In an open learning environment the learners naturally spread themselves over the range of the curriculum, each requiring instructionally relevant data, and each demanding considerable managerial attention from you, the teacher.

Records must be kept on the learner during the instructional process so that subsequent educational decisions can be made by either the learner, you or the administration. The record keeping and record generation functions of CML must therefore be divided into the events that best reflect both your and the organization's necessary management functions within the open learning setting. At the most fundamental level these functions are instructional, course and programme functions. The most important of these is the desirability of providing an inventory of learning experiences to the learners to maintain an awareness of their own status. CML generates large amounts of data that is manipulated and stored in such a way as to serve two functions, that of indicating learner strengths, difficulties and progress and validating test items, objectives and instructional materials.

CML AND ON-LINE LEARNING

You can set up your assignments for your on-line learning environment in a number of different ways using the CML system. For example, you can have the system generate a number of different kinds of assignment including tutorials, in-course assessments and pre/post-tests.

In an on-line learning environment it is important that you have as much interaction as possible to ensure your learners have the opportunity to 'practise' the skill and better understand the materials. It is also important that your CML tutorials have no prerequisites, meaning that learners can attempt a tutorial without having to complete any other tutorials. This allows learners to interact with topics out of sequence if they wish.

Other CML assignments such as in-course assessments and pre- and post-tests should assess the various topics in your learning event. In-course assessments usually have a different course map from the tutorials and you should require your learners to complete the relevant tutorials before you allow them to complete your in-course assessments. You will also need to consider allowing your learners to attempt the CML pre-test just once as its aim is to determine what objectives your learners have already achieved. The post test, of course, can only be completed after the tutorials and in-course assessments have been completed.

SAMPLE COURSE DESIGN

Following is an example of a typical CML course map or testing strategy. The course has eight tutorials, two in-course assessments and a post-test. The topics and tutorials are as follows.

Course: Algebra

1   Whole numbers
2   Decimal fractions
3   Integers
4   Linear equations
5   Measurement 1
6   Measurement 2
7   Factoring
8   Algebraic fractions

The course map for this course is shown in Figure 9.1.

Figure 9.1   *Course map*

The numbers 1 to 8 indicate the individual CML tutorial. IC 1 refers to in-course assessment 1 and IC 2 refers to in-course assessment 2.

The map shows that learners can complete tutorials 1 to 4 in any order, then they must complete IC 1. Once IC 1 is passed the learners would then complete tutorials 5 to 8, again in any order. The second in-course assessment, IC 2, would then test the learners' knowledge of tutorials 5 to 8.

The post-test measures the learners' knowledge of all the tutorials. However, before it can be attempted the learners must have 'mastered' all the tutorials and passed the two in-course assessments.

CATEGORIZATION OF TEST ITEMS

Start by developing a small test bank so that you can field trial the course map. Once this is successful then you can expand the test bank.

The items for different types of CML assignments can be drawn from the same or different test banks. Test banks can be assigned to different levels of difficulty and test items can be drawn from those different levels. The levels used to store test items can be based on their degree of difficulty or on the basis of the type of CML assignment in which they are going to be used.

For example, you could use level 1 to store test items for all your CML tutorial questions, level 2 for the CML in-course assessment and level 3 for the post-test. Test items can be drawn from different levels for one CML assignment.

If each of your tutorials has five objectives and you want to draw four questions for each objective, the course map can be designed as follows:

- tutorials: draw all questions from level 1
- in-course assessments: draw all questions from level 2
- post-test: draw all questions from level 3.

A second alternative is to draw test items from different levels as follows:

- tutorials: draw two questions from level 1
                draw two questions from level 2
                draw one question from level 3.
- in-course assessments: ten questions from level 1
                            five questions from level 2
                            five questions from level 3.

Drawing the test items from different levels has the advantage of giving learners exposure to a more realistic testing environment as they are able to see and work with different types of test items.

The size of your item bank is also a factor that you will have to take into consideration when you are designing your assignments. It is important when developing item banks to remember a couple of specific rules. First, for security reasons a large number of items limits the number of learners who are presented with any one item. Second, the minimum number of items in the bank should be controlled by two factors: assignment length and the total number of learners to whom an item may be administered. For example, if your exam is 100 items long an adequate bank size would be 600 to 800 items. On average an item should only be presented to 10 to 15 per cent of your students and on average the overlap between items administered to any two learners should not exceed 15 to 20 per cent.

CONCLUSION

Computer managed learning systems bring major benefits to those of you involved in their use. CML systems provide continuous feedback to your learners and tell you how they stand at the conclusion of the various learning events. Many CML systems 'diagnose' learner strengths and weaknesses and some systems allow for remediation and enrichment to be included as part of your test item answer comments. For the most part you, as a teacher, are relieved of many lower level management tasks that are automated by the CML system.

Your knowledge of your learners is greatly enriched by purposeful reporting of information relevant to decision making, and your capacity to control complex and rapidly changing procedures for the individualization of learning is also greatly enhanced. Similarly, your freedom from involvement in the processing of large amounts of data allows you more time for interaction with your learners. Using CML, administrators have rapid access to information on course registration, learner progress and resource use that better informs a range of administrative decisions. Instructional developers and course designers also have continuous access to vital information for both formative and summative evaluation of their innovations. Finally, course delivery options become more flexible as your learners are able to access learning materials in different ways.

Chapter 10
Delivering On-line Learning Materials

SUMMARY

Using the World Wide Web as a 'library' of appropriate learning information means that the learner can access and retrieve various materials deemed necessary to foster learning. Not only can you use the Web as a library, you can, of course, put up your own materials in a variety of forms that learners can access as the need arises. The Web can be used to give a lesson, deliver a slide show and/or show a short video clip. Using various structures and links, you can design interactive learning experiences for the learner whereby they share information with you the facilitator.

This chapter outlines the various considerations needed to deliver Web based learning materials to learners to ensure the materials meet their learning needs.

INTRODUCTION

The World Wide Web has great potential both as a library of learning resources and as a presenter and processor of learning materials. For example, if you want to develop your learning materials other than as a text based book you can create a a Web based 'book' that changes during the learning event in response to learner input. This interactivity makes for a more dynamic approach to learning when transferring the learning to a new situation.

A Web based learning event can be designed to use a particular instructional method and can use different elements of computer based learning. You can present 'live' content as well as making content both self paced and self directed. You can also provide up to the minute information that can be delivered immediately almost anywhere in the world.

WHY USE WEB BASED LEARNING?

Using the Web to deliver your learning event(s) has a number of advantages.

There is *increased learner accessibility* – placing learning materials into a Web environment can save both time and resources and provide an archive for learners who were unable to attend class or who misplaced their notes.

In a traditional environment a 'distance learner' often required a great deal of time to receive learning materials and communicate with the school, college or university providing the course. Using the Web as an information distribution system the learner can access the materials as soon as they are placed on the server. You can also set up a system to tell your learners when materials have been added so they can investigate the changes.

An essential part of any learning experience is communication. Make sure that your on-line classroom provides facilities that support a number of types of communication.

The Web environment allows you to design and develop information and presentations independent of software packages or a computer platform. Typically, learning materials using a multimedia or multiple media approach are designed using applications such as Authorware, Director or Tool Book. This means that the learner's computer must contain a copy of that software in order to display the materials. The problem is, however, that not all computer platforms are the same, not all Web browsers are the same and not all computers have the resources to make the presentation work effectively. All of which makes for a less than effective learning experience for the learner. Using the Web as a delivery platform along with an appropriate format for the learning event enables the materials to be independent of application software and computer type. However, you will still have to ensure that your learner's computer has a browser capable of displaying the materials and that your materials are in a format that can be used by all.

There is *increased learner effectiveness* – in the face-to-face classroom, an effective learning event is typically conducted in lock step fashion where learners are considered to be homogeneous and the

A Web based classroom is not the solution to every problem you may face with your class. It does have limitations that must be considered before you start building your on-line system.

materials appropriate for all. Using a Web based system, however, you can consider the diversity of the learners in terms of experience, skill, reading level, overall ability and attitude by offering different explanations, remediation of various kinds and an opportunity for the learners to proceed at their own pace.

Resource and reference materials of all types can be placed on-line and made accessible. Information can be made searchable using indexing programs and utilities allowing all learners to have equal access.

Because of the ease of putting materials on-line and providing options for the learner, appropriate amounts of supplementary information can also be placed into your Web distribution system. These materials might include troubleshooting guides, 'how to' manuals and other auxiliary information. Finally, with respect to increased learner effectiveness, you can create and embed cross links and reference links into your text and graphics to enhance learning.

There is *administrative support* – the Web can also be used to set up a variety of support features including electronic bulletin boards and other 'chat' facilities to enable your learners to keep up with changing course and materials information. Also in the context of a typical school, college or university, the Web can be set up to distribute administrative information including test results, tutor lists, timetables, grades, announcements and other resources such as past examination papers.

Advantages of the Web

Make sure that you strike a balance between learning and the technical principles so your on-line classroom serves its educational purpose.

Overall the use of the Web in learning can increase learner effectiveness and learner accessibility to learning by widening the potential client base. Through the judicious use of learning materials designed to enhance and not overwhelm learning, learner and teacher satisfaction can be achieved. Cost savings can also be realized in the use of the Web as an organizational administrative tool.

One of the major advantages of the Web is the ease of updating materials. Materials subject to change such as regulations and legislation, for example, or other materials with a short shelf life, in the past posed a problem with respect to placing those materials into a format that could be changed or adapted when needed. Even with the advent of the read, write CD ROM, retrieval posed and still continues to pose a problem, because of system incompatibility. The Web, however, is the ideal place to 'store' volatile materials to serve as a valuable resource for the learner.

Disadvantages of the Web

The Web does, however, have a number of disadvantages. The first and most obvious is speed. The network to which the learner has access may not be fast enough to support the materials you want or need to provide to the learners. Both audio and video files can take up huge amounts of file space and 'fancy' graphics can take considerable time to download to the learner's screen.

The second major disadvantage is equipment. As noted previously not all learners have access to the latest Whiz Bang, Super Mega Hertz, Inter Galactic, Power Tower from the Whiz Bang Computer Shop touted in magazines, newspapers and by the 'computer set'.

In fact, many learners are at the low end of the latest whiz bang machine, unable to run the latest Web browser and frustrated when they have to wait considerable time to download a relatively small file.

Overall the Web is still an expensive place to be. Setting up and maintaining a Web based classroom requires technical support, use of equipment and software packages and your learning materials still require significant time to design, develop, write, implement and maintain.

COMPUTER PLATFORM

In order to ensure that your virtual classroom is able to support the learning materials and the learner, as well as ensure that communication and interactivity is a standard feature, you could design your own application. To do this, however, you would need a large group of specialist staff and equipment, or you could have a commercial organization develop it for you. Your third option is to use an off-the-shelf product that has a number of customization options and set it up in your organization. Before you decide on the off-the-shelf application there are a number of basic questions that you need to ask yourself. These questions include the following.

All Web based classrooms need technology support. Make sure that the technology you choose is appropriate, familiar and ready to do the job.

- What is the rationale?
  - Why is the system being designed this way?
  - Why is it being developed at all?
  - Is there a better way to develop the system and if so what is it?
- What features do I need?
  - chat room(s)?
  - break out rooms?

      – discussion area?
      – assignment area?
      – laboratory area?
      – materials delivery options?
- Do I want to include Computer Managed Learning in the system?
- What resources do I have available?
      – Is the organization able to support the system?
      – Does the organization have the people needed to support the system?
      – Is the organization committed to supporting the system over the long term?

Some of the commercially available software includes Top Class, Lotus Learning Space and Persyst. Each of these applications has different attributes that you need to assess based on the needs of your learners and your organization.

DESIGN AND DEVELOPMENT CONSIDERATIONS

As part of your delivery options you will have to give some thought to the design and development of the actual materials. The first consideration you will have to make is how and where you are going to use on-line or Web based learning. On-line learning events can replace 'traditional' instruction in each of the following areas:

- learning at a distance
- open learning and/or self study
- supplementing current lectures
- replacing current lectures
- missed lectures
- examination revision
- supplementary examinations
- projects/assignment work.

If you are considering supplementing your current lectures or tutorials you may wish to consider using on-line learning in the following scenarios

- as introductory 'nice-to-know' information that would typically be delivered in a mass instruction mode

- in cases where the message is repeated a considerable number of times so as to ensure consistency and more efficient use of facilitator time
- to help the remedial learner by presenting the materials in a variety of different ways and introducing diagnostic tests to help learners be more aware of their standing with respect to those materials.
- in areas where collaboration is needed between learners materials can be designed to require active participation and interaction through on-line discussion and chat rooms.

Basic design considerations

When designing on-line learning materials you should follow a formal instructional design model and start by determining your learner's needs. (The first book in this series, *Planning A Course*, provides a full review of the various planning tasks that should take place prior to the design, development and delivery of learning materials.)

Design considerations include:

Remember that a number of tasks performed in a Web based classroom suit a more sequential presentation structure.

- choosing a delivery methodology for each portion of your learning curriculum based on the learner objectives. Do not make your delivery choice based on the technology just because it is there
- make sure that your materials design keeps learners involved with the materials. Active involvement helps ensure that learning will occur
- try to offer your learners alternative delivery modes. For example, if the learner can't grasp the concept in print perhaps he or she can follow an audio or video file
- develop a variety of templates such as structured, non structured, presentation, troubleshooting and adaptive guides for the learners to use as they proceed through the materials. Using a formalized structure in this way will help learners choose the correct path through the learning materials.

Screen design considerations

It is very important that your screen design is an effective interface between the learner and what has to be learned. To help in this regard keep the message as simple as possible. Your electronic text has to complement messages being delivered in other ways such as face-to-face delivery or as an audio file. The electronic text should not repeat everything being said. Use a maximum of seven points per screen and try to limit those points to the minimum number of words possible. Following these simple rules will help keep your screen uncluttered.

When dealing with visuals you should keep them as simple as possible. For example, try to centre them on the screen and always place them next to the related text. Use captions when it is appropriate and line drawings to show or highlight the details of an object. Keep your visuals simple by removing all the non-relevant information.

Try to use orientation devices to help the learner chart his or her path through the learning event. Use a maximum of two sub headings and use bold or colour for emphasis, but don't over do it! Use bullets for lists and use numbers for procedures.

When it comes to colour the recommended colours for screen based text are green, red, blue, magenta, cyan, yellow and white. Green, white, yellow and cyan can be used for text on a dark background.

Some recommended colour combinations are shown in Table 10.1.

Table 10.1   *Recommended colour combinations for screen based text*

Text	Background
White	Magenta, red, green, blue
Yellow	Blue
Cyan	Blue
Green	Yellow
Magenta	Blue, white
Red	White, yellow, cyan
Blue	White

Combinations to avoid include:

- yellow on white, green or purple
- red on black, blue or green
- magenta on green or black
- green on white
- blue on black
- blue on green

Try not use dark text on a bright background. The contrast may be good but the brightness of the display can make reading difficult. You can also use colour to highlight a graphic object in a diagram or graph. Differentiate data sets on graphs and group objects in a diagram by displaying them in the same colour. Do not use colours in ways that contradicts their conventional meanings. For example, red would not be a good choice for an 'all clear' signal. Remember too that colour has different uses and meanings in different cultures, for instance the appropriate colour to display at a funeral in a Western society is black whereas in a Chinese culture it is white. Make sure that you do your research before reaching your final colour decisions.

The psychological meanings of colour also varies among cultures, individuals and social classes. Table 10.2 shows some of the more common meanings for colour.

Table 10.2 *Common psychological associations with colour*

Colour	Meaning
Black	Boldness, professionalism
Green	Nature, growth, money
Red	Stop, importance, danger, error
Yellow	Cheerfulness, happiness
Blue, green	Calm, serenity, trust, cold, forbidding

PHYSICAL DESIGN

When considering the physical design of your learning materials keep the following points in mind.

● Keep each of your screens consistent in layout and overall design. Keep the same background unless you have a very good reason for changing it.
● Ensure that the text on the screen is legible. Make sure that the font you are using is a serif font and is at least 12 point. Keep in mind, however, that when you are dealing with fonts that the size of a particular typeface does not relate to the actual size of the printed image.
● Use both upper and lower case text. All upper case is difficult to read and could be misconstrued as emphasizing something that need not or should not be emphasized.
● Use a single column of text and try to restrict the use of frames.
● Keep the text left justified with a ragged right.
● Keep your line lengths to 60 characters or less.
● Break lines at the ends of words rather than using hyphens.

- Indicate paragraphs by leaving an additional blank line rather than indenting.
- Break long passages of text into different screens rather than having the learner scroll down the page.

CONCLUSION

This chapter has discussed the use of the Web to store and deliver learning materials. The chapter reviewed the potential of the Web as a tool to deliver a learning event along with its advantages and disadvantages. Also covered was the platform you will need to deliver learning materials and a number of design and materials development considerations.

Further Reading

Bell-Gredler, M E (1986) *Learning and Instruction: Theory into practice*, New York: Macmillan.

Bergstrom, B A and Stahl, J A (1992) *Assessing existing item pool depth for computer adaptive testing*, San Francisco, CA: National Council on Measurement in Education.

Brewer, I M (1985) *Learning More and Teaching Less*, University of Guildford, SRHE & NFER–Nelson.

Brownell, G (1992) *Computers and Teaching*, 2nd edn, New York: West Publishing Company.

Bruh, P and H Guthrie (1991) *Designing Learning Guides for TAFE and Industry*, South Australia: TAFE National Centre for Research and Development Ltd.

Cole, P G and L K S Chan (1987) *Teaching Principles and Practice*, Englewood Cliffs, New Jersey: Prentice-Hall.

Davies, B G (1993) *Tools For Teaching*, San Francisco, CA: Jossey-Bass.

Gagné, R M (1977) *Conditions of Learning*, 3rd edn, New York: Holt, Rinehart & Winston.

Hartley, J (1981) 'Eighty ways of improving instructional text', *IEEE Transactions on Professional Communication*, vol. 24, no. 1, pp. 17–27.

Hartley, J (1985) *Designing Instructional Text*, 2nd edn, London: Kogan Page.

Hodgson, V E (1993) 'Educational computing: mirrors of educational values'. *Educational and Training Technology International*, vol. 30, n. 1, pp. 32–8, February.

Holmberg, B (1980) *Essentials of Open Learning* (A course on open learning), Hagen: Fernuniversitat, ZIFF.

Holmberg, B (1989) *Theory and Practice of Open Learning*, London: Routledge.

Hsu, J and Fong J *et al.* (1993) 'Exploratory learning environments: what are they and do learners explore', *Journal of Educational Computing Research*, volume 9, number 1, pp. 1–15.

Jonassen, D (1982) *The Technology of Text*, 2nd edn, Englewood Cliffs, New Jersey: Educational Technology Publications.

Juler, P (1990) *Promoting Interaction, Maintaining Independence: Swallowing the mixture?* Open Learning, volume 5, section 2, pp. 24–33.

Keegan, D (1990) *Foundations of Open Learning*, 2nd edn, London: Routledge.

Kolb, D A (1984) *Learning: Experiences as a source of learning and experiential development*, Englewood Cliffs, New Jersey: Prentice-Hall.

Lewis, R (1985) *How to Develop and Manage an Open Learning Scheme*, Open Learning Guide 5, Council for Educational Technology, London: H Charlesworth & Co.

Lewis, R and D Spencer (1986) *What is Open Learning?* Open Learning Guide 4, Council for Educational Technology, London: H Charlesworth & Co.

Matthews, D (1982) An infrastructure for continous intake individualized education [and] infrastructure for learning management, Austin, Texas: *National Institute for Staff and Organizational Development's Annual International Conference on Teaching Excellence and Conference of Administrators.*

Race, P (1984) *The Open Learning Handbook: Promoting quality in designing and delivery flexible learning*, London: Kogan Page.

Race, P (1994) *The Open Learning Handbook,* London: Kogan Page.

Rogers, D F and Smith, P R eds (1994) 'Case Studies in CAL!' *Computers and Education* volume 8, number 1 pp 35–39, 101–25, 133–44, 151–8, 179–81, 203–11, 219–24.

Rowntree, D (1990) *Teaching Through Self-instruction*, revised edition, London: Kogan Page.

Rowntree, D (1992) *Exploring Open and Distance Learning*, Open and Distance Learning Series, London: The Open University.

Wilson, B (1987) *Methods of Training and Individualized Instruction*, Study Skills, volume 3, Training Technology Programme, Carnforth: Parthenon Publishing.

Wilson, B (1987) *Methods of Training Resource-based and Open Learning*: Study Skills, volume 4, Training Technology Programme, Carnforth: Parthenon Publishing.

Yoshikazu, A (1992) 'CMI system for evaluation of learning results' in Saunders, D and Race, P eds *Developing and Measuring Competence,* London: Kogan Page.

Index